Love, Liberation, and Escaping Slavery

Love, Liberation, and Escaping Slavery

William and Ellen Craft in Cultural Memory

BARBARA McCASKILL

THE UNIVERSITY OF GEORGIA PRESS   Athens and London

A Sarah Mills Hodge Fund Publication

This publication is made possible, in part, through a grant from the Hodge Foundation
in memory of its founder, Sarah Mills Hodge, who devoted her life
to the relief and education of African Americans in Savannah, Georgia.

Parts of the introduction, chapter 3, and chapter 4 were previously published in substantially
different form in "The Profits and Perils of Partnership in the 'Thrilling' Saga of William and
Ellen Craft," *MELUS* 38, no. 1 (2013): 76–97; reprinted by permission of the Society for the
Study of the Multi-Ethnic Literature of the United States. Parts of chapter 1 and chapter 2
were previously published in slightly different form in "Ellen Craft (ca. 1826–1891): The
Fugitive Who Fled as a Planter," in *Georgia Women*, vol. 1, edited by Ann Short Chirhart and
Betty Wood (Athens: University of Georgia Press, 2009); reprinted by permission.

Set in Adobe Caslon Pro by Graphic Composition, Inc.
Printed and bound by Thomson-Shore
The paper in this book meets the guidelines for
permanence and durability of the Committee on
Production Guidelines for Book Longevity of the
Council on Library Resources.

Most University of Georgia Press titles are
available from popular e-book vendors.

Printed in the United States of America
19 18 17 16 15 P 5 4 3 2 1

Library of Congress Control Number: 2015932616

ISBN-13: 978-0-8203-3802-6 (hardcover)
ISBN-13: 978-0-8203-4724-0 (paperback)
ISBN-13: 978-0-8203-4832-2 (ebook)

British Library Cataloging-in-Publication Data available

For my charismatic mom and dad,
Mrs. Inez Owens McCaskill and Colonel John L. McCaskill Jr.,
two of the freest people I have known, who taught their children
to face the South and to honor family members lost and found.

And for Nancy Grayson. Your encouragement, enthusiasm,
and sharp, attentive questions kept me focused and moving forward.

Contents

Acknowledgments   *ix*

Introduction. The Crafts and the Memory of Slavery   *1*

One. The "Thrilling" Escape of William and Ellen Craft from Georgia   *14*

Two. Boston's Glorious Fugitives   *34*

Three. Running a Thousand Miles *in England*   *55*

Four. The Boston Libel Trial of William Craft   *75*

Epilogue. A Story to Pass Down   *87*

Notes   *93*
Bibliography   *107*
Index   *127*

Acknowledgments

This book, like the story it tells, is the progeny of both opportunities and setbacks. In researching and writing it, I have experienced generous portions of frustration and laughter. The late, brilliant Elizabeth Fox-Genovese provided insights and words of encouragement that set me on this journey many years ago. I owe its completion to an expert, creative, hardworking team at the University of Georgia Press that includes Walter Biggins, senior acquisitions editor; Bethany Snead, assistant acquisitions editor; John Joerschke, project editor; Chris Dodge, freelance copy editor; Mick Gusinde-Duffy, editor-in-chief; and Lisa Bayer, director. Formerly of the press but not forgotten for their enthusiastic and thoughtful endorsement of my scholarship are Nicole Mitchell, Nancy Grayson, and Sydney DuPre. The informed and thoughtful critiques of John Ernest and DoVeanna Fulton, who served as anonymous reviewers, helped me polish and refine drafts of this book. David E. Des Jardines, director of marketing, also has my gratitude, and his earlier inspirational work identifying illustrations for the University of Georgia Press's Brown Thrasher Books edition of *Running a Thousand Miles for Freedom* merits my belated appreciation.

I have benefited from space to think, support for research travel, and the occasional course release to catch up with reading and writing as the recipient of institutional grants from the University of Georgia

Research Foundation, the Willson Center for the Humanities and Arts, and the University of Georgia's Office of the Vice President and Provost for Academic Affairs. I have been the delighted beneficiary too of a Hugh Kenner Elsewhere Award from the University of Georgia's Department of English.

At Radcliffe Institute for Advanced Study, Harvard University, a 2004–5 Augustus Anson Whitney Fellowship inspired a turning point in my project and led me to connections I previously had overlooked. I extend Christine DeLucia of the Radcliffe Institute Research Partners Program very warm thanks for her impeccable library sleuthing and critical reader's eye. The Radcliffe Institute Fellowship Program, under the visionary leadership of Drew Gilpin Faust and Judith Vichniac, arranged public presentations of my project. Members of their staff connected me with Virginia Craft Rose, Angela Niles, Virginia Niles, and other descendants of William and Ellen Craft, making a very pivotal year of study and reflection even more unforgettable. I fondly remember Tiffani Williams, Irene Pepperberg, and Barbara Savage for their supportiveness and companionship at Radcliffe Institute, and I will not forget the optimism, humor, wisdom, and can-do spirit of the late Lindy Hess.

Shorter residencies of several months facilitated my immersion in print and online archival collections pertaining to the conductors, funders, and passengers of the Underground Railroad. These were funded by the W. E. B. Du Bois Institute, Harvard University, directed by Henry Louis Gates Jr.; the Aaron Diamond Foundation and the Schomburg Center for Research in Black Culture, New York Public Library; and the Gilder Lehrman Institute of American History (for study at the Columbia University Rare Book and Manuscript Library). I am very thankful for the patient and knowledgeable staffs at all of the university libraries and research repositories I visited who assisted me and gave me direction and leads. The following people offered encouragement and interventions beyond the call of duty: Catherina Slautterback, curator of prints and photographs, Boston Athenæum; Georgette Mayo, reference archivist, Avery Research Center for African American History and Culture, Charleston, South Carolina; Diana Lachatanere, former curator, Manuscripts, Archives, and Rare Books Division, Schomburg Center for

Research in Black Culture, New York Public Library; Muriel Jackson, head, Genealogical and Historic Room, Washington Memorial Library, Macon, Georgia; Krystal Appiah, reference librarian and curator of African American History, Library Company of Philadelphia; Beatrice Greene, formerly of the Rare Books and Manuscripts Department, Boston Public Library; and Elizabeth Bouvier, head, Massachusetts Supreme Judicial Court Archives. I extend heartfelt thanks to Julia Ellen Craft Davis for her generosity and swift agreement to my use of Craft-Crum family photographs in this book.

Additionally, this book has been shaped by conversations with colleagues at summer research programs sponsored by the American Antiquarian Society and the National Endowment for the Humanities. I am ever in the debt of Richard Brown, who directed an NEH Summer Seminar on "Early American Microhistories" at the University of Connecticut, for serving as a patient sounding board as I brainstormed and tweaked the arc of my study one summer month. The three dynamic directors of the NEH Summer Seminar on "The Role of Place in African American Biography"—Frances Jones-Sneed, Richard Courage, and Robert Paynter—organized one of the most supportive, multidisciplinary, and able communities of literary critics, historians, theorists, social scientists, and other scholars I have encountered in my career. Jonathan Hartmann, Reighan Gillam, Joy Myree-Mainor, Jennie Lightweis-Goff, Martha Pitts, Kenith Matthews: thank you for the coffee shops, campus tours, inspiration, and fellowship!

As the Fall Semester 2012 Fulbright Visiting Chair of Society and Culture at Dalhousie University, I lived in Halifax, Nova Scotia, where the Crafts fled from American slave catchers in 1850. Deborah Lawrence created a comfortable, inviting, memorable home away from home. I miss her homemade ginger tea and kitchen conversations on the lore of Atlantic Canada and politics of African Nova Scotia, as well as my second family of Jenny Kang, Phil, Lionel, and Mr. Mittens. For their hospitality and cultural insights, I can sing the praises of these members of Halifax's academic community: Afua Cooper, Bruce Greenfield, Marjorie Stone, Anthony Stewart, Julia M. Wright, Judith Thompson, Trevor Ross, Dominic Silvio, Carole Poirier, and Mary Beth MacIsaac, all at Dalhousie University; Sylvia D.

Hamilton and Elizabeth Edwards, University of King's College; Phanuel Antwi, St. Mary's University; and Henry Bishop, Nova Scotia Community College. Back in Georgia, Jordana Rich, Stacy Turner, and my wonderful neighbors relieved my worries and reassured me that all was well on the home front during my travels.

Many questions I have asked about the African American archive have been answered by conversations, emails, and phone calls with experts in nineteenth- and twentieth-century African American and Afro-Caribbean literature and culture. In no particular order, I'd like to recognize the following scholars, accountability partners, draft readers, letter writers, coaches, cheerleaders, critics, and marathoners, whose candles have lit my own and who have modeled how to do good work: Rhondda Robinson Thomas, Koritha M. Mitchell, Sharon McCoy, Jeffrey Green, Eric Gardner, Will Ginn, Barbara Ryan, Lois Brown, Ezra Greenspan, Jürgen E. Grandt, Spenser Simrill, Joycelyn Moody, Lee Roy and Freda Scott Giles, Timothy B. Powell, John Inscoe, Ed Pavlić, Kent Leslie, Valerie Levy, Hugh Ruppersburg, Ann Short Chirhart and Betty Wood, Carolyn Sorisio and Martha Cutter, Michael McDermott, James C. Hall, Christine Levecq, Doris Kadish, Dale L. Couch, David W. States, Valerie Babb, Kelly Caudle, Lesley Feracho, Katherine E. Flynn, John Wharton Lowe, Martine Watson Brownley, Rosemary Franklin, Judith Ortiz Cofer, P. Toby Graham, and two colleagues and fellow academics who have passed on and whose advice I have sorely missed: Richard Newman and Aaronette White.

I would like to single out individuals and institutions on both sides of the Atlantic who invited me to present public lectures or keynote addresses about William and Ellen Craft and advanced my research through their astute feedback: Sarah Robbins and Linda Hughes, Texas Christian University; Caroline Gebhard, Loretta Burns, and the Fanny Richardson Cooley Interdisciplinary Forum, Tuskegee University; MaryNell Morgan, Paul and Mary Liz Stewart, and Manisha Sinha, Underground Railroad Public History Conference, Russell Sage College; Anita J. Ponder, Andy Ambrose, and the Tubman African American Museum, Macon, Georgia; Sharon L. Moore, University of Nevada, Las Vegas; and Jane Hiles Collins, Samford University, London Study Centre.

Thank you, patient friends and supporters Cecilia and Jorge Rodriguez Milanés, Weihua and Qiwei Zhang, Sonja and Paul Lanehart, Jane Barroso, Roberta Fernandez, Nancy Felson, Melinda L. de Jesús, Sylvia Hutchinson, and Aghigh Ebrahimi Bazaz. If I have forgotten to recognize you, please forgive my omission and know that I cherish you very much for championing this project and moving me forward to its completion.

Finally, I am blessed by Spyder who believes in the power of play, and for family members who have kept the faith and kept calling and texting even when I didn't answer the phone or respond right away: Sandra and Mark Hill, Brenda and David McCaskill, Amanda and Chris Hill, Mom, and Samantha Hill, M.D.

Love, Liberation, and Escaping Slavery

The Crafts and the Memory of Slavery

A quarter of a century ago, William and Ellen Craft were
slaves in the State of Georgia. With them, as with thousands of
others, the desire to be free was very strong. For this jewel they
were willing to make any sacrifice, or to endure any amount
of suffering. In this state of mind they commenced planning.
After thinking of various ways that might be tried, it occurred
to William and Ellen, that one might act the part of master
and the other the part of servant.
—*William Still, "Female Slave in Male Attire" (1872)*

This book begins with Harlem and an umbrella. A few years out of
graduate school, I accepted a one-semester fellowship at the Schomburg Center for Research in Black Culture, New York Public Library.
Like a modern-day sphinx majestically poised on Malcolm X Boulevard, placidly witnessing the neighborhood bustle beneath a wide sky,
the Schomburg Center boasts of being one of the world's largest repositories of manuscripts, visual materials, and other cultural productions of the peoples of the African Diaspora.[1] Along with the beloved
Apollo Theater at 125th Street, gleaming Strivers' Row down West
138th and West 139th Streets, and—underneath all of that—the "A"
train up to Lenox Avenue that Duke Ellington and his orchestra im-
mortalized in 1941, the library is a breath-taking, enchanting place of
pilgrimage, a siren's song for lovers of literature and letters like me.

Although Europeans sought to dominate the Americas during
centuries of slavery and the slave trade, the holdings of the Schomburg Center shed light on the fact that diasporic African communities kept alive and transformed the expressive African traditions of
literature, music, dance, oration, theater, and art. This creativity also

buffered the horror that James Baldwin, writing one hundred years after the Emancipation Proclamation, designated as the "invented reality" of American identity during slavery and Jim Crow: a "fantastic" invention, as he called it, supported by "the Bible and the gun," that offered access and belonging to "everyone" even as it excluded African Americans from such attainments.[2] The Schomburg Center especially beams approval upon and pays tribute to the pantheon of artists, writers, and musicians of African descent whose hangouts during the New Negro Renaissance of the 1920s and 1930s were the libraries and living rooms of stylish upper Manhattan. They included Jacob Lawrence, Aaron Douglas, Claude McKay, Countee Cullen, Jessie Fauset, the musical team of Eubie Blake and Noble Sissle, James Weldon Johnson, James Rosamond Johnson, Bob Cole, Dorothy West, and one-time collaborators and coauthors Zora Neale Hurston and Langston Hughes.[3] Hughes's ashes are interred in the Schomburg Center, beneath a floor painted with African cosmograms, a mandala, and the quotation, "My soul has grown deep like the rivers"—the final line from his signature poem "The Negro Speaks of Rivers" (1921).[4]

Rather than on these luminaries, my residency at the Schomburg was focused on conducting research about African American women who wrote and lived during the nineteenth century. I had been looking for a literary idiom that appealed to my interests in American society and culture, and in feminist literary and critical theories that articulated the social edges of African Americans' activism and our collective responses to the additive, intersecting dimensions of institutional systems and structural policies that had historically oppressed or negated us.[5] I thought I had found this idiom in the spiritual narratives of formerly enslaved African American men and women. Yet, as I considered these narratives as subjects of scholarly research, I also found myself challenged by the complexities and variations within the genre. In terms of such elements as lengths and scopes of the narratives, the direct or indirect perspectives of their narrators, the times and places of their publication, their targeted readers, and the genders and religions of their authors, such memoirs varied widely. However, like many a fortunate or foolhardy scholar before me, these complexities proved minor deterrents to my investigations.

Riffling through the card catalog, a tactile and auditory experience that is a relic of what it meant to be a researcher before the explosion of Internet databases and electronic finding aids, I developed an extensive list of titles that I had fallen behind in reading, thanks to a dissertation deadline and then the subsequent demands of a full-time tenure-track position at a large public university. I filed away for future analysis the occasional single-authored religious and conversion narratives I discovered, the spiritual memoirs of formerly enslaved women and free women of color recovered by (and continuing to capture the imaginations of) such scholars as Marilyn Richardson, William L. Andrews, Joycelyn Moody, DoVeanna Fulton, Reginald Pitts, Carla L. Peterson, Chanta M. Haywood, Lena Ampadu, P. Gabrielle Foreman, Frances Smith Foster, Rafia Zafar, Yolanda Pierce, Katherine Clay Bassard, and Henry Louis Gates Jr. As I shuffled through the catalog drawers, I also lingered over a different kind of slave narrative: the 1860 book *Running a Thousand Miles for Freedom*, by "Georgia Fugitives" William Craft (1824–1900) and Ellen Craft (1826–91).

Yet the Crafts didn't attract my full attention until one very rainy day in late winter toward the end of my fellowship. I had procrastinated about getting forms notarized for my new appointment at the University of Georgia, which would begin in just a few weeks. After a quick review of addresses involving another old-fashioned, offline ritual—letting my fingers do the walking through Yellow Pages—I located a notary public in law offices just opposite the building where I then resided, near the border of Washington Heights and Sugar Hill in Upper Manhattan. Spring was still several weeks away, yet the air felt as sodden and thick as during the heat and humidity of a Georgia July. Rain flared down in gusting sheets as I dashed from my apartment building, then skated and slid across the street, my oversized umbrella proving more hindrance than help. Bursting through a door on the other side of the street, I entered a blessedly dry and warmly lit vestibule. Beyond, an orderly office decorated with elegant, formal furnishings seemed transplanted from the magnificent Harlem parlor of heiress and businesswoman A'lelia Walker (1885–1931) or from the fictional uptown soirées in the novels of Jessie Fauset (1884–1961) where the bohemian culture vultures of Harlem's Niggerati, as Zora Neale Hurston (1891–1960) called them, "proclaimed . . .

the undiluted good of all things Negro" as they floated in "courageous clothes" through tastefully appointed chambers.[6] A courteous African American woman greeted me, then gazed intently at my red-and-black umbrella, whose colors she instantly identified as the University of Georgia's. I had not encountered many people in the Big Apple who had visited or even heard of the University of Georgia, in spite of its storied football team, legendary Sanford Stadium, and star running back Herschel Walker, and his renowned coach, Vince Dooley. Why such familiarity with the school and the state? She was distantly related, she replied, to two former Georgia slaves: William and Ellen Craft. By just a few months, it turned out, I had missed the celebration and reenactment of the Crafts' 1850 marriage at a Schomburg Center event studded with food, music, and family and neighbor reunions.

This was my summons to enter the world of the Crafts—their writings and their speaking tours, their antislavery and educational activism, the public and private tests that defeated them, and the transatlantic networks that sustained them. During my remaining tenure at the Schomburg Center, I attempted to learn as much as possible about the long arc of the couple's actions on behalf of love and liberation: their dramatic escape from slavery in central Georgia, their participation in antebellum New England reform movements, their exile to Great Britain punctuated by the publication and reception of their 1860 narrative, and their project to educate the freedpeople in the Georgia low country. One year later, I had composed an essay on Ellen Craft that *African American Review* published as "'Yours Very Truly': Ellen Craft—The Fugitive as Text and Artifact." In it I discussed Ellen's appearances on the transatlantic stage: on the dais with William at antislavery lectures and meetings, in public letters and reports in the press, and arm-in-arm with white British reformers at London's Crystal Palace in 1861. In addition to the famous engraving of Ellen attired as a southern white slaveholder, the audacious and clever disguise she conceived in order to facilitate her escape with William from bondage, I explained how presentations of her body suggest cultural norms regarding respectable femininity and how they hint at obstructions she and William faced as an African American man and woman attempting to strike a middle ground between the guidance of white and black abolitionists and their own decisions and preferences.

Despite their romantic story of escaping together from slavery, William's later adventures as a merchant to western Africa, and their travels across three countries and three continents, scholarly and artistic discussion of the Crafts were scant after the Harlem Renaissance. Carter Godwin Woodson (1875–1950), the educator and scholar who founded February's Black History Month celebration, published a story about the handsome couple for grammar-school curricula in his didactic *Negro History Bulletin*, as I will discuss in chapter 1 of this book. Additionally, during the 1930s, the poet and playwright Georgia Douglas Johnson (1880–1966) tried and failed to get the Federal Theatre Project to adopt the script of her historical play titled *William and Ellen Craft* for inclusion in a national program that encouraged theatrical productions with social protest themes.[7] Then in the late 1980s two groundbreaking, meticulously researched, biographical essays on the Crafts, still essential reading for researchers embarking on thoughtful study of the couple, were published by the historians Dorothy Sterling and Richard J. M. Blackett.[8] For the most part, the Crafts seemed more conducive to the instruction, edification, and entertainment of general audiences than the scrutiny of intellectual ones.

William and Ellen Craft are unforgettable, so their rise and fall in popularity over the generations may reflect that their lives have not neatly aligned with English-speaking audiences' assumptions about how African peoples functioned in bondage, and with the kind of man and woman they were expected to become in freedom. Why have they been so atypical? Their escape together, their family together, and their work and activism together exemplify what Frances Smith Foster identifies as "stories of African American collaboration" that have been "less well known in our culture than those of the rugged individualists who succeeded against the odds." "Particularly in the narratives of African American cultural history before Emancipation," she writes, "the lone fugitive, the fiery rebel, the singular sojourner, or the inspired visionary dominates our attention. Our narratives of racial progress generally feature a heroic Moses while making

it seem that half of his challenge was convincing those he would res-
cue that if they would stop acting like crabs in a barrel, they could
become people with a purpose."[9]

The Crafts also deviate from images pervading cultural memory of
enslaved Africans toiling in the fields or trudging among the cabins
of the slave quarters. Relative to other bondsmen and bondswomen
around them in plantation hierarchies, both of them benefited from
a degree of mobility and autonomy. Additionally distinguishing the
Crafts from most other American fugitives, once they escaped from
Georgia they resided in England, and they lived longer there than
they remained in nominal freedom in the American North. However,
they did not leave the South forever, vowing never to return, but instead retraced their steps to live and work in coastal Georgia a few
years after the Civil War. They were energetic, intrepid, tenacious, and
industrious people, yet neither Ellen nor William dedicated themselves to the vocation of writing, as did Frederick Douglass (1818–95)
or, as Ezra Greenspan labels him, their "imaginative and versatile" ally
and advocate William Wells Brown (1814–84), who would relentlessly
"write, recite, orate, perform, sing, and debate his opposition to the
physical, mental, and spiritual violation of his people."[10] Other pursuits, equally absorbing and socially committed, occupied the Crafts.
Finally, the devastating conclusion to their public story, one that unfolded in Georgia, from where they first lit out for freedom, resists the
triumphal ending we attach to many other fugitives' lives.

To understand when and how the Crafts began to attract more attention, it is useful to turn to the research and reflections of the historians Waldo E. Martin Jr. and Peniel E. Joseph on the subject of more
contemporary African American communities. Both Martin and Joseph have written extensively on the nationalist functions of literary
and cultural productions in the twentieth-century African American
freedom struggle. Martin states that postwar African American activists of the 1950s, 1960s, and 1970s recognized how "culture and cultural work are central."[11] Like the artists of the New Negro Renaissance, they poured their energies into conceiving dynamic poetry,
theater, music, and art that examined themes of freedom, identity,
nationalism, community improvement, and race and racism. As Joseph writes, their creative outpouring attained its apex and apogee

with the Black Arts Movement (1968–75) and its emphasis on African American pride and self-esteem, political action, and "poetry and race consciousness." Youth at the vanguard of the Black Arts Movement pushed back against what they identified as a systemic, intentional miseducation about American history, society, and culture, and the deliberate academic and social tracking or ghettoization of students of color into vocational rather than college preparatory courses. They also took historically black educational institutions to task for placing elitism over principle and largely turning a blind eye to problems in working-class and poor black communities.[12] The African American students developed coalitions across racial and ethnic backgrounds to take over administrative offices and stage walkouts together. They demanded more black teachers and administrators, and they protested against the insufficient number of courses focused on black literature, culture, and history.

In response to one such action by students in Philadelphia's public, private, and Catholic schools, the actors Ruby Dee (1922–2014), who played Lena Younger in the acclaimed screen version of Lorraine Hansberry's *A Raisin in the Sun* (1961), and her husband Ossie Davis (1917–2005), who famously eulogized Malcolm X at his 1965 funeral, traveled to the city to shoot *Now Is the Time* (1967), a documentary about black nationalism as an empowering historic response to racism and racial violence.[13] From the segregated lunch counters of the downtown sit-ins to the integrated buses of the interstate freedom rides, it had not taken long for black youth to mobilize and to go viral with their critique of urban community schools that purported to educate students and to invest them with the skills to succeed in a competitive workplace, yet measured far short of the mark. Such activism rekindled a hunger to investigate early African American literature and culture, and to bring to this fresh endeavor an old awareness of how narratives of earlier African Americans were battlegrounds for agency, resistance, and self-respect, rather than merely sad old sagas of victimization and oppression. Publishers such as Books for Libraries Press and AMS Press rushed to meet the renewed demand for African American writers by identifying and reprinting slaves' narratives and other early literary productions by African Americans that lay forgotten in campus library collections and research repositories.

The Pulitzer Prize–winning novelist Alice Walker, for example, began her recovery project on Zora Neale Hurston in the late 1970s after an African American literature class during which she had read *Mules and Men* (1935), Hurston's collection of black folklore from the Deep South. Her emotions were stirred by Hurston's commitment "to the survival of her people's cultural heritage," only to have been excluded from the African American literary canon based on "misleading, deliberately belittling, inaccurate, and generally irresponsible attacks on her work and her life by almost everyone."[14] By facilitating what the landmark anthology *All the Women Are White, All the Blacks Are Men, but Some of Us Are Brave* (1982) announces as an agenda of "revising the Black woman's role in slavery, recovering Black female oral and popular culture, and revamping the reputations of earlier Black women authors," Black feminist projects such as Walker's investigation of Hurston helped to make early print publications visible and accessible.[15] As P. Gabrielle Foreman and Reginald Pitts observe, the African American text *Our Nig* (1859) is one rediscovery from this "black women's literary revival" that also marked an uptick in black women's literary and cultural creativity.[16] It had been long awaited, one of many changes that the soulful Sam Cooke had prophesied in his music, but by the late 1980s the climate became conducive again for scholars and teachers and readers to move the slaves' narratives, including William and Ellen Craft's *Running a Thousand Miles for Freedom*, from the invisible, silent margins of American literature, where they had been hiding in plain sight, to the center of scholarly investigation.[17]

In books by Florence Freedman (1989), Cathy Moore (2002), and Judith Bloom Fradin and Dennis Fradin (2006), the slave narratives were introduced to new generations of young Americans and popularized as educational reading. The cover of *The Brave Escape of William and Ellen Craft* (2006), a graphic version of their story marketed to such readers, presents the two fugitives as strong, fearless, and unflappable. They are pepped up and prepared for action. Ready to roll, Ellen bursts out of their cabin door like a powerful feminist superhero. Meanwhile, a steely-eyed William glances out of the page as if emboldening—and daring—the youth who read about them to join their pioneering journey. The "delicious expeditions" to "unknown countries beyond the seas" and solemnly sworn pacts to "never separate to death" that spice such perennial children's favorites as *The Adventures of Tom Sawyer* (1876) by Mark Twain (1835–1910) are brought to mind by the cover of *The Brave Escape*.[18] The separations, hair-trigger decisions, and near detections that the Crafts endure on their nerve-wracking journey to freedom, and the self-control, trust, and faith they must maintain in order to stay free, invite children to draw the lesson that, like these two heroes, one day they may face challenges, heartaches, heartbreaks, and limitations that test whether or not they have what it takes to make their most cherished dreams come true.[19]

As Marlene D. Allen and Seretha D. Williams write, "The slave narrative is the foundation of the African American prose tradition. Its themes of authenticity, freedom, hunger, literacy, faith, [and] captivity, and the techniques of irony, propaganda, and realism inform and define an explicitly African American literary tradition."[20] In addition to reflecting topics and rhetorical styles of such pre–Civil War slaves' narratives, *Running a Thousand Miles for Freedom* anticipates postbellum African American novels that, according to Robert Reid-Pharr, express deep misgivings and discontents about the all-American dream of belongingness and assimilation, even as they also play to this theme.[21]

In my study that follows, I track themes of love, liberation, and escape during four extraordinary moments of the Crafts' public lives of service and activism: their flight from slavery, their second flight (from slave catchers in New England), the years in Britain surrounding the publication of their memoir, and their post–Civil War project of establishing schools in Georgia to educate the freedpeople and prepare them for agricultural employment. In addition, my analysis of both their memoir and its paratext ventures how the Crafts and their antislavery friends framed and remembered the fugitives' story to both challenge and conform to cultural attitudes, and how, in the shifting nature of such expectations, they may have planted the seeds of their undoing. To these ends, I refer specifically to reports and advertisements published in both antislavery and commercial transatlantic newspapers, legal records, personal and public correspondence, visual images, private correspondence, census and burial records, speeches, minutes of antislavery society meetings, and essays and memoirs written by white Britons and Americans who interacted with the couple through covert Underground Railroad networks or committees and alliances in reform movements. I seek to answer the calls of scholars of African American literature and early American print culture to move the focus of our critical investigations beyond a preoccupation with what Eric Gardner describes as the primacy of "the bound book as the measure of literature," the result of misleading perceptions of eighteenth- and nineteenth-century African American printed productions as scarce, inaccessible, and unreliable.[22]

This book emerges out of broader conversations by scholars of African American literature, American print culture, and the history of the book about the current challenges of investigating and recovering early African American literature. "With African American texts," Foster has written, "as with other cultural material produced by and for other devalued groups, so much has already been lost, gone astray, or been stolen that complete restoration is impossible. Even the seemingly simple task of creating an inventory of extant nineteenth-century newspapers and periodicals seems an existential endeavor." Foster has argued persuasively that when frustration about a paucity or incompleteness of sources is not the issue, then a failure to understand that "[e]arly African American print culture . . . is virtually synonymous with the Afro-Protestant press," with the work of publishers like the A.M.E. Book Concern (1817–1952) and of publications like the *A.M.E. Christian Recorder* (founded 1852), has caused contemporary researchers to overlook them. This has led to what she and Gardner describe as an over-absorption by researchers with how early African American texts respond to the slavery issue and racism, which runs the risk of overlooking how they have framed educational, entrepreneurial, and political agendas.[23] Another outcome of narrowly defining what early African American literature looks like and who early African American writers might have been is to neglect those productions written in languages such as French, Spanish, and Arabic, and those productions influenced by Islam and other world religions besides Christianity.[24] Finally, the disciplined and probing work of Elizabeth McHenry, as well as that of Gardner,

Leon Jackson, and others, has reminded us of how little we know and how seldom we ask about who read African American literature, and their scholarship has advanced methods of tracing such communities of readers through subscribership and circulation data and fostered private and public discussions of the sharing of printed texts.[25]

Discussing her own archival research of the novelist and editor Pauline Elizabeth Hopkins (1859–1930) and the teacher Susan Paul (1809–41), Lois Brown writes that "scholars of African American literature and culture . . . can enrich biography by attending to the published materials—novels, collections of poems, plays, songs, art, and speeches—and by scrutinizing and courting the public materials—newspapers, city directories, maps, shop and stock inventories, census reports, wills, and legal documents."[26] In addition, she has called for the creation of "models of inquiry and critical expectation" that can mine unpublished writings and correspondence and personal objects such as scrapbooks and autograph albums for insights into early African Americans' personal and public experiences.[27] As Gardner advises, researchers must undertake such investigations by beginning from the premise that much of the early African American archive is partial or missing.[28]

I have wrestled with such contingencies in my own biographical explorations of the Crafts. For example, no personal correspondence between the couple has been uncovered, nor have letters, diaries, journals, or other published or unpublished reminiscences that recall firsthand what either of them may have thought about the other. Moving toward a fuller understanding of their lives has included "reading through the lines and against the grain of compromised sources," as Jackson observes in his call for new scholarship about African American printers.[29] It has meant learning how to read and recognize the contradictions and silences in the famous engraving of Ellen Craft fleeing slavery as a southern planter, as well as the handful of other images of her and William.[30] It has meant looking in sources other than books for examples of their own writing and speech, and decoding the observations and reminiscences of both American and European allies and detractors in order to separate these perceptions and expectations from the possible aspirations, motives, and opinions of the couple themselves. It has demanded that I seek to understand how the Crafts' cross-racial collaborations come to life both in their published memoir and in what Beth A. McCoy identifies as the paratextual spaces or "epigraphs, dedications, prefaces, and other bookish elements" throughout African American cultural productions.[31] By defining archival sources expansively, we can recognize the choices that the Crafts and other fugitives faced as they juggled activist goals in partnership with antislavery friends and their own agenda for their family and for their fellow African Americans seeking freedom.

The collaborative nature of the Crafts' public experiences, their activism in North America, Great Britain, and Africa, and the absorbing paratextual evidence that surrounds them add up to an enduring, significant story. While my book is not a full-blown biography, it contemplates pivotal and white-knuckle moments in the couple's lives that made a cultural imprint during abolition and Reconstruction. In the spirit of approaching an incomplete early archive as generative rather than thin, my study also intends to point future researchers to additional paths of literary and cultural investigation. What opinions, for example, did the Crafts frame about each other? Where do early archives and oral histories of the couple in Africa take their story? How did postbellum African American leaders in the South receive the former fugitives, and at what cost did the Crafts maintain independence from such institutional levers for the freedpeople's education as the Society for the Propagation of the Gospel and the American Missionary Association?

In recovering the work of the novelist Julia C. Collins (ca. 1842–65), William L. Andrews was reminded of "countless African Americans—both men and women—doing important work in their communities, whose names and deeds were not widely recorded and recognized, and who remain unknown to us today."[32] A forgotten manuscript or discarded image promised immeasurable insights into such early change agents and culture workers. What we know about the Crafts and their quests for connection and autonomy in and out of slavery performs the cultural work of memorializing those other unrecorded, unrecognized souls, and it points us to a process of inquiry as tantalizing and tangled as their story. For myriad cultural purposes, audiences down the generations have loaded onto the Crafts both dreams and anxieties of race and freedom, yet William and Ellen are more complex than that. Out of the patchwork of their memories and ours, finally, emerges a story of devotion and persistence borne out of confronting oppression and caring for family together, and of together committing their energies to the abiding liberation of African peoples.

CHAPTER ONE

The "Thrilling" Escape of William and Ellen Craft from Georgia

On arriving, the warm hearts of abolitionists welcomed
them heartily, and greeted and cheered them without let or
hindrance. They did not pretend to keep their coming a secret,
or hide it under a bushel; the story of their escape was heralded
broadcast [*sic*] over the country—North and South, and
indeed over the civilized world.
—*James Williams,* The Life and Adventures
of James Williams *(1873)*

Appearing for two decades as writers and speakers to transatlantic
American and British audiences, William and Ellen Craft would re-
iterate themes of unattained liberty and unfulfilled promises of citizenship. They would perform a balancing act of revelation and disclosure that simultaneously connected them to and distinguished them
from others who had formerly been enslaved. Their intertwined story
is thus a recitation of paradoxes and contradictions: lives mediated
by privilege even as they suffer enslavement's sorrows; independence
and assertion constrained by the expectations of abolitionist benefactors; public displays of masculinity and femininity that run counter
to private gender roles; attitudes of disclosure that collide with secrets
and lies about their histories in and out of slavery.

In October 1937, working from the nation's capitol, Carter Godwin Woodson commemorated the pair in the very first issue of his
Negro History Bulletin. Now known as "the Father of Black History,"
Woodson had inaugurated Negro History Week in 1926, a forerunner
of today's Black (or African American) History Month. A Harvard-

educated visionary and professor who also had taught high school students, Woodson dedicated his scholarship to uplifting the masses of African Americans by recovering and celebrating their myriad past achievements that had been suppressed, ridiculed, undervalued, or forgotten. Even earlier, on September 9, 1915, Woodson had cofounded the Association for the Study of Negro Life and History (ASNLH). During a time of separate-and-unequal schools and exclusion from all-white organizations, it served as an oasis for African American educators and intellectuals.[1] Likewise, part of a shifting, multifaceted project to arrest what Woodson termed the "mis-education of the Negro," his compendious *Negro History Bulletin* was intended to instill racial pride, to invigorate individual and community achievement, and to inspire African American students and teachers at the elementary and secondary levels with the sense of a glorious past and a glowing future destiny.[2] "The Thrilling Escape of William and Ellen Craft" was the cover story of the first issue of *The Negro History Bulletin* (see figure 1).

Woodson was familiar with the story of the Crafts. In one of his books he reprinted a letter in which, writing from England, William Craft tells the American reformer Samuel J. May (1797–1871) about his and Ellen's progress in learning to write and their desire to obtain an education in order to assist in emancipating their people still enslaved throughout the American South. Woodson had also uncovered and published a letter by William Craft that references the publication of *Uncle Tom's Cabin*.[3] He and *Negro History Bulletin* coeditor Arthur N. Brooks very likely had calculated that the youthful vigor of the "smart, polite, courageous" William and the "gentle, beautiful" Ellen, their intense affection for each other, and their suspenseful adventures would appeal to an audience of school-aged readers.[4] The account of the Crafts in *The Negro History Bulletin* reinforces popular images of the couple as victorious heroes and attentive lovers by summarizing, paraphrasing, and quoting liberally from a flattering essay published in *The Underground Rail Road* (1872), a massive book compiled by the black abolitionist William Still (1821–1902).

Had they been alive to read it, William and Ellen Craft might have been tickled by the neat litany of triumphs and successes that the *Bulletin* story organized for its youthful audience. Rather than a

THE NEGRO HISTORY BULLETIN

Published Monthly

Vol. I.   No. 1.   WASHINGTON, D. C.   October, 1937

The Thrilling Escape of William and Ellen Craft

ELLEN CRAFT

WILLIAM CRAFT, a smart, polite, courageous young man, and Ellen, a gentle, beautiful young woman, were slaves on the same Georgia plantation. Their master knew they loved each other, so he gave them permission to marry.

One day, William said to his wife, "Ellen, our master has allowed us to marry. But in slavery we can never really be man and wife. We do not belong to each other. We belong to our master. We are his property. He can sell us whenever he wishes. We are happy now, but tomorrow, you may be sold away from me, or I may be sold away from you. Our happiness may end at any moment. There is only one way to avoid this. In some way we must become free."

"I understand you perfectly, William," said Ellen, "but there is no way for us to be free. Why worry about things which you cannot change? You cannot destroy slavery. Those slaves who have tried to strike down their owners have failed. Uprisings which they have planned have been checked at the start. A few slaves have worked hard for years and with their savings have purchased their freedom. Occasionally others have been freed by kind masters whom they have rendered faithful service. A number of fugi-

tives, following the north star and assisted by friends, have reached the land of freedom, but tears come to my eyes when I see that all these ways seem closed to us."

"I have the idea," said William. "It came to me last evening when I was asleep. We shall run away."

"How shall we do it?" asked Ellen.

"I have solved the problem of our freedom," said William. "Here is how we'll do it. You will dress up like our young master in one of his suits. You will have your hair cut like that of a young man. You are fair enough to be taken for white. Ellen, dear, you will look like a young planter elegantly dressed in a cloak and high-heeled boots."

"Freedom is dear," said Ellen, "and we should do everything possible to obtain it; but how can a woman stand such a long and hard journey from Macon, Georgia, to some northern point in New York, Massachusetts or Canada? How can I continue pretending that I am a man when I am questioned at close range or when I am approached as if I were a man?"

"That will be easy," said William. "Muffle your face as if you were suf-

fering from a toothache. This will prevent people from finding out who you are. This will also keep persons from knowing that you haven't a beard."

"That sounds all right for the traveling from place to place," said Ellen. "But what about stopping here and there for food and shelter? There are well-to-do free Negroes in Charleston, Richmond, and Baltimore, but a 'young white master' could not safely stop with them. He would be taken for one of them. Many free colored people are almost white. We shall have to stop with white people or at hotels. How can I register at one when I can neither read nor write?"

"I have thought of that, too," said William. "You will put your right arm in a sling, limp a little with a cane in your left hand, act as if you were injured on the way, pretend that you are a little hard of hearing, keep these green spectacles over your eyes, and show that you must depend upon me, your servant, for everything you want. The clerk will sign the hotel book for you, and will let me stand by to give you close attention."

WILLIAM CRAFT

Ellen agreed to make the dash for freedom. The clothes were brought, the carriage was prepared, and they decided to leave on the following Saturday. This would give the runaways forty-eight hours to travel before their escape would be known. There was to be a holiday from Saturday evening until Monday when they would be missed for the first time.

Ellen was ready at the appointed time. She looked like the young master. William, full of pluck and natural ability, was a fine, strong man. He was very attentive to his "young master." He was eyes, ears, hands and feet for "him." Ellen had little to say or to do except to attend to the "ailments" which she was supposed to have and to act like a master. She would not accept acquaintance with those attracted to her and would pretend to be deaf while William, the "servant," explained the illness of the "young master." Many instance of the kind occurred, but William was always ready to make an explanation which prevented closer approach with his "master."

"We are now approaching a city," said William. "This is Charleston. I know a little about this place. My master once brought me here as his servant."

(Continued on page 5)

ON THE WAY TO FREEDOM

Figure 1. William and Ellen Craft ride intrepidly to freedom in this story from the inaugural issue of *The Negro History Bulletin* (October 1937). Used with permission of the Association for the Study of African American Life and History www.asalh.org.

linear narrative, where triumphantly they traversed from slavery to escape to liberation, their real-life saga had been a recursive one. The account in *The Negro History Bulletin* reinforces how, as John Ernest writes, "the stories told about the Crafts, from their first appearances on the antislavery lecture circuit to accounts of their lives long after they died, reflect a deep cultural need to find resolution and meaning in the complex historical story of the American system of slavery."[5]

A sort of triptych of the Crafts frames the first *Negro History Bulletin*'s cover page: three woodcuts designed by Howard University's Lois Mailou Jones (1905–98), a gifted artist then on the verge of international fame. A member of the art faculty at Howard University, Jones submitted her original illustrations to books printed by Woodson's company, the Associated Publishers, Inc., during the 1930s and 1940s. She valorized the cultural contributions of African Americans by synthesizing European and African aesthetics in her watercolors, sketches, and oil paintings. One month before the publication of "The Thrilling Escape," fed up with the racism of America's art world, she sailed to Paris for a prestigious installment in the Académie Julian.[6]

Jones's portraits of Ellen, dressed like a gentleman, and her husband William gaze from each of the *Bulletin*'s upper corners, their nerves and energies galvanized by their commitment to flee from slavery together. A foreshortened image of the anxious Crafts hastening "on the way to freedom" in a horse-drawn buggy barrels out of the page's bottom center. One is invited to hear the wooden carriage wheels as they rumble over cobblestoned streets and to sense the nervous tension of the fugitives. The engine of their progress is not so much a horse as it is all of the countless escaped and freed slaves who preceded them. As Ellen tells William in this story, "A few slaves have worked hard for years and with their savings have purchased their freedom. Occasionally, others have been freed by kind masters whom they have rendered faithful service. A number of fugitives, following the north star and assisted by friends, have reached the land of freedom, but tears come to my eyes when I see that all these ways seem closed to me."[7] Ellen verbalizes a mood of mingled hope and despair, action and paralysis, that characterized many African Americans from the eras of the triangular trade, slavery, and Jim Crow through the King years of the civil rights movement. At a time in American history, nearly seventy-five years after emancipation, as African Americans raged mightily against the major and minor indignations of segregation—from urban centers like Woodson's home of Washington, D.C., to rural Deep South towns such as Washington, Georgia—Woodson's retelling of the Crafts' escape did more than merely celebrate freedom.[8] It advised young African Americans of their legacy and urged them to take up the liberation struggle their ancestors had begun and bring it to completion.

Because of a roving husband and the revenge of a humiliated wife, by the late 1840s Ellen had occupied an advantageous, although inferior, position in a wealthy Macon, Georgia, household. Her life began on a cotton plantation in Clinton, Jones County, in the crucible of American slavery, near what was then the state capital of Milledgeville. She was born in 1826 to Major James P. Smith, her white master, and to his house slave Maria, who herself was half-white. As the master's daughter, Ellen was exempted from slogging sunup-to-sundown through exhausting field labor, yet she was the child of rape, that "greatest indignity" of slavery imposed upon slave women and their families.[9]

In his essay "Rape in Black and White," Norrece T. Jones Jr. concludes, "No aspect of slavery, other than ownership itself, was more widely and consistently condemned by former slaves—or those most familiar with them—than the sexual violence that so many of them had to endure."[10] As an enslaved woman, Ellen Craft's dreadful future might consist of sexual assault by her owner and/or other white males who held dominion over her body; resentment and abuse at the hands of her white mistress; and shame, guilt, or even contempt on the part of her black husband, slave or free, who would be helpless to protect her so long as some white person retained her as property.

For the Crafts, Ellen's nettling and dangerous identity as her southern master's daughter and property would set into motion a sequence of events climaxed by the two of them meeting, marrying, and welcoming a new year on the freedom side of the Mason-Dixon Line. Embarrassed and outraged by the frequency with which Ellen was mistaken by visitors and neighbors as a white child of her own, the "tyrannical" Mrs. Smith removed Ellen completely from her service, scorn, and sight.[11] Instead of selling her, she presented Ellen in April

1837 as a wedding present to Ellen's eighteen-year-old half-sister, Eliza Cromwell Smith (1819–79). Ellen was then eleven years old.

William was more reticent about his infancy and childhood than Ellen was concerning hers. His story with Ellen has been remembered in contemporary literature and oral histories largely as that of a bondsman possessed of visibly African features who escaped with his wife, an enslaved woman, who dramatically passed for a privileged white southern planter. The locket photograph reproduced in figure 2, like a photograph of a smartly dressed and erect William Craft documented by historian Kathryn Grover, affirms descriptions of this half of the "Georgia fugitives" as a man of evident "African extraction."[12] While nineteenth-century slaveholders and abolitionists who talked about him acknowledged his biracial identity alongside Ellen's (see figure 3), this aspect of William appears in the twentieth century to have been minimized or overlooked. For example, neither R. J. M. Blackett's extensive essay "The Odyssey of William and Ellen Craft" nor Dorothy Sterling's "Ellen Craft: The Valiant Journey," two seminal, rich, and carefully documented biographical discussions of the couple, delve into William's origins as a mulatto or mixed-race person.[13] On the other hand, the *Georgia Telegraph* of February 13, 1849, reprinting a story from the *New Haven Register* about the recently escaped Crafts, described the pair as a "good-looking mulatto man, and a still better looking, almost white girl, with straight hair."[14]

Throughout his career as an abolitionist, William would fall silent on the details of his mixed-race ancestry. This may have been another variation of the ex-slaves' stock profession to have very little recollection of birthplace, childhood, and family—which would be in line with the dehumanizing, traumatizing, anti-domestic effects of slavery.[15] By tamping discussion of the brown-skinned William's Caucasian heritage and foregrounding Ellen's blended ancestry, activists like the Crafts could highlight the sexual victimization of enslaved women. They could slant William as a nineteenth-century hero whose African blood challenged white male monopolies on such traits as bravery, pride, and intellect. Additionally, descriptions by the antislavery press of the 1840s and 1850s of William's mulatto identity may have reflected racial and cultural biases that "logically" attributed precocious or positive actions to European blood, even as

Figure 2. Locket with image of William Craft, from William and Ellen Craft's photograph album (ca. 1850s). Craft and Crum families collection. Photo courtesy of the Avery Research Center for African American History and Culture, College of Charleston, South Carolina.

they attempted to lessen the stigma of maladjustment and inferiority assigned to African ancestry. In his book-length study titled *Drama, Theatre, and Identity in the American New Republic* (2005), Jeffrey H. Richards identifies the racism of abolitionists as a rationale for William and Ellen's discomfort with emphasis on his mulatto features:

> As recent scholars have shown, New Englanders, however much their good intentions, their sympathy with plantation slaves, and their general shift towards abolitionism may have carried them, nevertheless retained a significant repulsion for blacks as people and as a presence in their increasingly provincial culture. For every John Greenleaf Whittier or even William Lloyd Garrison—who, as his conflicts with Frederick Douglass indicate, had his own long education to undergo with regard to the beings he ostensibly fought for—there are many more "Yankees" without forceful interests in the welfare of African Americans, the Nathaniel Hawthornes, for instance, who virtually erase blacks from the written map of their reflected consciousness. Even in the 1850s, the only represented blacks with any dignity on stage are mulattos, quadroons, octoroons, near-whites whose only tragedy is not being all white.[16]

Figure 3. Ellen Craft, from William and Ellen Craft's photograph album (ca. 1850s). Craft and Crum families collection. Photo courtesy of the Avery Research Center for African American History and Culture, College of Charleston, South Carolina.

In response to such prejudice against blacks and blackness that soured their hopes of attaining full respect and acceptance from many white northern allies, William and Ellen Craft may have deliberately downplayed William's mixed-race pedigree. As the literary scholar P. Gabrielle Foreman writes, their pushback declared a militant "rejection of white superiority and affirmation of racial loyalty," even as white abolitionists who were nervous about and threatened by such pride undermined them by suppressing publication of joint representations of the striking couple, black man and "white" woman.[17]

What William did recall again and again in his written and oral accounts is having witnessed his own loved ones auctioned off to settle the debts of his first master, a merchant named Craft, who saw to it that William was trained as a cabinetmaker. In quick succession, the businessman accrued too many debts from cotton speculation, declared financial insolvency, sold William's parents and siblings, and handed William, then in his midteens, to a Macon accountant named Ira H. Taylor, whose bank held the mortgage on his property. Taylor paid half his purchase price. In one of slavery's customary ironies, Dr. Robert Collins, the physician, financier, and entrepreneur who had married Ellen's "white" sister Eliza, paid the other.[18]

Collins had emerged as a scion of Macon business and society. The Central Georgia town, the largest in the state's interior, was in high gear and swiftly ascending to commercial prominence. Cotton tufts swirled in the air as ponderous trains hissed in and out of the city, with their lucrative loads and compartments of gawking passengers. The melodic sounds of market women mingled with the rhythmic chants and grunts of work gangs, and the students of Georgia Female College (now Wesleyan College) strolled on the campus lawn while beyond them in the wide, known world others cranked the pulleys and pumped the bellows and pistons that powered the Industrial Age.

Georgians regarded Macon as a hub of transportation for the middle and western portions of the state and as a magnet for educational and business ventures, which Collins had been influential in creating. He was a booster for the railway system that linked ginned cotton and other crops produced in Georgia's interior to the growing and ever-hungry cities along its perimeter—especially to the cosmopolitan Savannah, which long had been a destination for the ships of the transatlantic slave trade, and which, by the mid-1840s, could lay claim to the title of the busiest commercial seaport on the southeastern coast.[19] Collins was also a cofounder of the Monroe and Bibb Railroad and Banking Company, a spearhead of train service in Macon during the 1830s and 1840s. In addition to his medical practice, he earned his money through investments, agriculture, entrepreneurship, and finance. And slavery. The author of an 1852 essay on slave management, Collins owned sixty-two slaves by the early 1840s and over ten thousand acres of land.[20] Through Collins's ownership of their bodies,

William's life would intersect with Ellen's, and as Collins's property they would fall in love, court, and marry.

Ellen and her half-sister Eliza, like the home and grounds where they lived, were external indicators of Collins's social and financial successes and essential ingredients to the running of his household and the rearing of his heirs. Ellen's primary duties were as "a ladies' maid" to Eliza, which probably included responsibilities such as assisting her mistress and other white women in the household in bathing, dressing, grooming, and maintaining their linens and wardrobe; straightening, cleaning, and organizing the female bedchambers and their contents; accompanying the ladies of the house to shops and on other errands; escorting them and other family members to visit neighbors; sewing, mending, and quilting; and supervising the mistress's children. "[A] favourite slave in the family," Ellen was even put up in "a little room to herself"—an astonishing privilege in a culture where the "bedroom" for a house slave usually meant a corner near the kitchen, a niche under the doorway, or a pallet within shouting distance of the mistress and master.[21] The historian Dorothy Sterling affirms how Ellen's unprecedented privacy was no fiction. She writes that the Collins family "permitted [Ellen] to move to a one-room cabin of her own, in the woods behind the big house, where she could keep bolts of cloth and sewing implements."[22]

Looking back decades later on their years in slavery, the Crafts pronounced Eliza Smith Collins "decidedly more humane than the majority of her class."[23] The resemblance of Ellen's and Eliza's names may reflect not only kinship, but a genuine, if guarded, allegiance that may have incubated during their childhood and intensified as both became women.[24] The Collins family subscribed to the customary practice of not permitting their human property the Christian sacrament of marriage vows sanctified by a minister. Yet in 1846 they did allow the Crafts to commemorate their union with the ritual of "jumping the broomstick."[25]

If Eliza played a role in approving the marriage, her intervention would have been another example of the favor she habitually bestowed upon Ellen. The historian Dorothy Sterling is skeptical that any love or affection could have existed between Ellen Craft, her half-sister

Eliza Smith Collins, and Eliza's mother, Mrs. Eliza Smith. She points out that Ellen was born during the same year that Mrs. Smith gave birth to a son named Elliott, his name suspiciously resembling Ellen's, which would have exacerbated the tensions and tempers among the black and white women of the household.[26]

What assessed in relative terms as a "more humane" relationship in *Running a Thousand Miles for Freedom* may therefore be a matter of expedience rather than sincerity, a calculated gesture to reassure their readership that slavery had not warped the black Crafts into haters of all white people. Even if there were no evidence of the racially inter-twined branches within Ellen Craft's family tree, I would hesitate to assume that the Collins's approval of the Craft's "marriage" ceremony was magnanimous or convivial. In her study *Life in Black and White: Family and Community in the Slave South* (1996), Brenda E. Steven-son identifies the power struggles between Eliza the mistress, Robert the master, and Ellen and William the enslaved that the Crafts' per-formance of "jumping the broom," often traced by scholars to West African sacred practices, also could have symbolized:

> "Jumping the broom," in fact, was a popular practice in early [pre-Christian] Anglo-Saxon villages where a couple jumped together across a broom placed in their family's threshold in order to signify that they entered the residence as husband and wife. . . . By imposing this cul-tural albatross on slaves, southern whites suggested the lack of respect and honor that they held for their blacks' attempts to create meaningful marital relationships. The slaves' acceptance of this practice, on the other hand, demonstrated the ability of slave culture to absorb, reconfigure, and legitimize new ritual forms, even those masters imposed out of jest or ridicule.[27]

William and Ellen Craft's daylight escape in 1848, directly under their masters' noses, would confirm their skills in playing the enslaved Af-ricans' game of cultural absorption, reconfiguration, and legitimiza-tion. Oppression had made them proficient in breaking down the walls of bondage and converting them into the stepping-stones of liberation.

As newlyweds, the Crafts initially decided to make the best of marriage in slavery, but their obsession with having children that no man or woman could own or sell formed the impetus for their escape.

The Christmas holidays would prove to be the ideal time for them to leave, when owners' restrictions on the movements of African Americans between plantations were often lifted or overlooked, when slaveholders were more congenial about granting passes to visit family and friends on neighboring plantations, and when slave patrols were likely to be distracted from their duties by the season's revelries. Their bold, risky, resourceful plan stemmed from Ellen's suggestion to employ her light skin to advantage by masquerading as an infirm southern gentleman planter.

"He" would say that he was traveling from Georgia to Philadelphia by the usual assortment of conveyances—rail, carriage, steamship—in order to seek medical treatment for various rheumatic ailments. To complete this ruse, Ellen would wear a hat and suit, cut her hair, tie bandages around her smooth face, hide her eyes behind green spectacles, and entwine a sling and a poultice around her right arm and hand. The brown-skinned William would dissemble as well, by pretending to be the devoted slave of his "master." [28]

In their memoir, William asserts that he proposed the idea of escaping in this way to a very reluctant Ellen. "After I thought of the plan," he says, "I suggested it to my wife, but at first she shrank from the idea." However, my research of the Crafts and their narrative contradicts his claim. The biography of William Wells Brown, the Crafts' friend and mentor and himself an escaped slave, published by his daughter Josephine (1839–?), contends that Ellen thought of the disguise. If Josephine Brown was right, then William's silencing of Ellen and revision of the facts in their 1861 narrative stands as an example of how black abolitionists often wrote formerly enslaved Africans into conventional gender roles. This meant representing African American women as deferential and submissive, and African American men as decisive and imaginative. [29]

On the eve of their escape the Crafts could barely read or write, as they "had, by stratagem, learned the alphabet while in slavery, but not the writing characters." William also reports how they were unable to read the travel passes they obtained to facilitate their flight, although years later, by claiming to have "learned to read a little" in spite of Georgia's legal policies barring whites from instructing slaves in literacy skills, he would muddy this statement about possessing only a glancing familiarity with the alphabet.[30] The extent of such illiteracy among enslaved persons like the Crafts, according to many experts, has been overestimated. In fact, the historian Steven Hahn estimates that very likely almost ten percent of southern blacks in slavery could read and write during antebellum years.[31] In pre–Civil War Macon, writes Donnie D. Bellamy, anti-literacy laws stipulated by the Black Codes were not always strictly enforced, so that "a number of" the city's enslaved people may have obtained a modicum of education.[32] Additionally, as the research of Janet Duitsman Cornelius suggests, those whites in Macon who did defy custom and law were more likely to give instruction in reading rather than in writing, "since slaves could write passes and run away, and also because writing was a skill which had not been traditionally allowed to the poorer classes."[33] Because Ellen was among the unlucky majority of enslaved people who were unschooled in reading and writing, the final touch of a sling for her arm was intended to help prevent recapture. Without the sling, her inability to write her name in registers might trigger the suspicions of hotel clerks and customhouse authorities on high alert to scuttle the schemes of runaways.

In the couple's own romantic version of events there is much left undisclosed about the realities and complexities of their lives in slavery. How did they obtain the money to purchase enough clothing and provisions for several days' travel and lodging on the way to the free states—and in case of unanticipated delays caused by adverse weather conditions, suspicious fellow travelers, or late or broken-down transportation? How did they learn the most efficient route from Georgia to the free states, and where to go and who to see when they got there? What loved ones did they have to leave behind?

After joining in union to Ellen, William had continued to work in a cabinet shop, which permitted him to engage in slavery's practice of "hiring out," in which enslaved men and women with sought-after talents made money for their masters by leasing their labor to other white employers in exchange for keeping a small cut of their wages. According to Hahn, "In cities like Baltimore, Richmond, New Orleans, and to a lesser extent, Charleston—or in agricultural processing towns like Danville, Lynchburg, and Farmville, Virginia, slaves usually fed and lodged themselves, bargained with prospective employers, and might receive payments for 'overwork.'"[34] In preparation for escaping, William stockpiled the earnings his master allowed him to keep. By waiting tables in exchange for his room and board, he saved even more money.[35] He very possibly worked his contacts in the cabinetry shop to his advantage by listening for information about escape routes and for northern sympathizers who might provide information and assistance, as well as acquiring additional garments to finish Ellen's disguise. Abolitionists report that she and William together "procured the necessary articles, buying one at one place, and another at another."[36]

For her part, Ellen was an expert seamstress who designed and sewed the pants for the black broadcloth suit she would wear. As Hahn reflects, "we may well have underestimated the extent to which slaves in a great many locales—with or without their owners' approval—may have bought, sold, and bargained with merchants, shopkeepers, peddlers, and neighboring whites."[37] Clothing, table linens, quilts, and bed coverings that Ellen may have stitched for this shadow economy, as well as for Macon's white elites, may have brought in additional funds to squirrel away for their escape. More tethered to her owners' home than William was to the shop, Ellen nevertheless may have been privy to knowledge of rail and steamer lines to take, places to stay, people to trust, and other important information from eavesdropping on the Collins's mealtime conversations and listening to the guests they hosted and the news they read aloud. "On individual holdings," according to Hahn, "women and children were particularly well placed to overhear discussions in the parlors, dining rooms, and immediate environs of their owners' residence."[38]

On the question of loved ones left behind, the Crafts maintained a public silence. There were a few exceptions they did mention: Ellen's grandmother and mother and William's immediate family members—father, mother, brother, sister—who had been auctioned on the block and scattered to the winds. Ellen's status as a favored house slave and the maternal interest of her half-sister and mistress may have barricaded her against the threat of rape or from being ordered to breed with other black men, even after she "married" the man she loved. Neither Ellen nor William ever publicly claimed children from their time in bondage. Yet, calling into question the romantic notion that William was Ellen's first husband or lover, at least two white male abolitionist colleagues, Reverend Theodore Parker (1810–1860), the eloquent Unitarian minister and Underground Railroad conductor, and a fellow Bostonian and Transcendentalist, the Unitarian pastor James Freeman Clarke (1810–88), would go public with a backstory about a child Ellen had borne in slavery, who died because she was commanded to abandon it until she completed chores and errands elsewhere.

Theodore Parker was a golden-tongued abolitionist with a fierce, direct, penetrating gaze, charismatic delivery, a global concept of social justice, and a single-minded devotion to taking down slavery. He invites comparison to such modern orators and change agents as the evangelist Billy Graham (born 1918), civil rights movement activist Fannie Lou Hamer (1917–77), and the forty-fourth US president, Barack Hussein Obama (born 1961).[39] He wrote the iconic handbills posted in Boston along the North Slope's narrow alleyways and lanes and slipped beneath the lintels of the African Meeting House and other gathering places, which admonished runaway slaves to beware of slave catchers and keep "top eye" open. His sayings have influenced generations of speakers and social activists who have followed him. For example, during the civil rights movement, Dr. Martin Luther King Jr. (1929–68) paraphrased a Parker adage when he said that "the arc of the moral universe is long, but it bends toward justice."[40]

Like many white men involved in American and British abolition, Parker was no stranger to the courts. He took a public stand on practicing civil disobedience against laws and legal policies that were anathema to his drive to emancipate enslaved African Americans. When summoned before the bench, he seized the opportunity to educate a captive audience about the savagery endured in bondage by fugitives like the Crafts. During the 1855 court trial of the fugitive from slavery Anthony Burns, Parker testified that "Ellen had a little baby,—it was sick and ready to die. But one day her 'owner'—for this wife and mother was only a piece of property—had a dinner party at his house. Ellen must leave her dying child and wait upon the table. She was not permitted to catch the last sighing of her only child with her own lips; other and ruder hands must attend to the mother's sad privilege. But the groanings and moanings of the dying child came to her ear and mingled with the joy and merriment of the guests whom the mother must wait upon. At length the moanings all were still."[41]

In the version recollected by James Freeman Clarke, an investor in the Crafts' Reconstruction-era vision to educate Georgia's freedpeople, the death of Ellen's child plays out under similar circumstances: her mistress orders Ellen to accompany her out of town, and the baby allegedly dies alone during her absence.[42] Clarke's and Parker's points were that slavery meant to deny women like Ellen what the scholar John Ernest describes as "the roles that define womanhood in America—the innocent woman, the devoted wife, the nurturing mother," and then to hold them in shame and contempt for not living up to these roles.[43] As concocted or exaggerated as this story of Ellen's baby may be, it is plausible that in their first two years of married life, before they lit out for the North, the Crafts may have lost a son or daughter by their own or other unions to any one of numerous maladies: malnourishment, miscarriage, the auction block, disease. The genealogist Katherine E. Flynn, for example, has uncovered that at least one Craft died in infancy, a two-year-old named Mary Elizabeth who succumbed in Boston in 1869, a few months after her parents had returned to America.[44]

In their melodrama and sentiment, such possibly apocryphal stories align with verifiable and unsubstantiated reports about enslaved children that white and black abolitionists commonly intercepted and reimagined in poems, antislavery hymns, and novels. Plots often feature a frantic field hand and mother whose imperious mistress forces her to abandon her nursing child. Hours later, the mother returns, only to discover her infant dead or wasting away at death's door from exposure, sickness, or some mortal wound inflicted by a snake or other wild creature.[45] With such imagined tales of the helplessness and heartbreak experienced by enslaved mothers and their children, American poets such as Lydia Sigourney (1791–1865) and Eliza Lee Follen (1787–1860) argued for the rights and well-being of women and African Americans and electrified feminist and antislavery sympathies. This influence was palpable in the "bitter shrieks" and "burden'd heart" that the poet Frances Ellen Watkins Harper (1825–1911) attributes to a mother whose child has been sold away; in a song that William Wells Brown collected describing a blind child rendered "helpless, forsaken, with strangers alone" as his enslaved mother drags to the coffle gang; in the famous *Uncle Tom's Cabin* (1852) of Harriet Beecher Stowe (1811–96), where the sale of her son Harry triggers the mulatto Eliza's iconic and desperate leaps to liberation across the icy Ohio.[46]

Implicating Ellen Craft in a similar catastrophe, whether she had actually experienced it or not, Reverend Theodore Parker and James Freeman Clarke in effect sealed her in what John Sekora identifies as the "white envelope" of abolition. Fugitive slaves who were of necessity beholden to whites for safety, shelter, food, funds, employment, and other assistance found themselves at risk of being controlled, condescended to, or, in the worst cases, exploited by their editors, publishers, or antislavery "friends."[47]

Having lived and worked around elite whites, William and Ellen would probably have known that within nineteenth-century norms of motherhood there was no absolution for an enslaved mother who abandoned her child, even if the fault lay in a master's unscrupulous whims and powers without limit. They would have known that this story of their baby entangled Ellen in a dilemma of desiring to claim the maternal qualities to which she was entitled and that respectable white society prized—innocence, devotion, nurture—yet standing accused of callously abandoning her child. They would have known, finally, that this story of their infant babe—apocryphal or not—threatened to place their self-described positions as pious, authentic Christians in jeopardy. What questions and suspicions about Ellen's modesty, William's manliness, and the binding ties of Ellen and William's love would arise if this dying baby had been fathered by her white master or even another enslaved or free African American man? In the stupefying and hypocritical logic and double standards of slavery, the burden of protecting her chastity and defending her virtue would have shifted from her owners to the enslaved woman herself, even if she had been sexually violated or threatened with punishments or sale for resisting her master's advances.

To meet the expectations demanded of them—mother and father, husband and wife, affectionate and monogamous Christian couple— the Crafts would stick to a public script about their relationship in slavery that suggested sexual abstinence or the application of birth control. They would insist on their decision to have children only after they made it to freedom, no matter that their friends would imply otherwise. So long as they depended upon the economic and social networks and the physical protections from bounty hunters that Boston's antislavery community provided, the Crafts would be fools to risk a disconnect between the upstanding people they presented themselves as being and the opportunists or slouches that a skeptical white public could easily think they were. Perhaps this explains why Parker spoke out publicly only after the Crafts had been tucked away in Britain for five years, and why Clarke waited even longer, until after the Reconstruction, to ante up his secrets in print.

Escaping from Macon, the alias that Ellen Craft used, "Mr. William Johnson," may reveal another portion of the couple's story that speaks to the power struggles within slavery and the psychological defenses that the enslaved erected against them. "Johnson," a ubiquitous, democratizing, one-size-fits-all American surname, like the slogan announcing "KILROY WAS HERE" from a different kind of war in a later century, functioned as camouflage for Ellen's true identity and to deflect suspicious second glances.

"Johnson" also surfaces in coded names developed by abolitionists who guided runaway slaves through the safe houses and personal connections that comprised the Underground Railroad. For example, in March 1849, the fugitive slave Henry "Box" Brown (born ca. 1815) shipped himself from Richmond en route to Philadelphia in a box that his friend Samuel Smith addressed to a "James Johnson, 131 Arch Street." "James Johnson" was a signal to antislavery friends who had been notified of Brown's plans, and who were waiting to receive the "shipment" at the warehouse of the Philadelphia, Wilmington, and Baltimore Railroad.[48] Ellen's combination of a generic surname, Johnson, with William's first name thus serves as a reminder of the sophisticated networks of information, shelter, people, and deception that supported the successful escapes of American fugitives, even though the Crafts did not travel from Georgia to the North on the secretive Underground Railroad. This ubiquitous, leveling surname may have nudged writers and readers in generations after the Crafts to pay attention to aspects of the couple's lives that conform to other fugitives' stories.

Behind Ellen Craft's hastily composed sobriquet, there may rest an explanation that speaks to the sectional struggles of slavery days. Growing up in Georgia during the 1820s and 1830s, both William and Ellen may have heard accounts of Colonel William Ransom Johnson (1782–1849), an affluent Virginia planter and gambler. Johnson, affectionately dubbed "The Napoleon of the Turf," was a national figure notorious for his devotion to horses, horse races, and horsemanship, and he was known far and wide for the dollars he lavished on these passions. He helped to establish horse racing as the first national sport, and he popularized what came to be known as the "intersectional match." In this Civil War fought symbolically from the saddle, a horse bred in the North and one raised in the South raced against each other for honor and bragging rights. On May 17, 1823, a few years before Ellen was born, Johnson put up a horse for the South, Sir Henry, against an undefeated nemesis, American Eclipse, owned by the New Yorker Cornelius W. Van Ranst. In front of a Long Island crowd of over sixty thousand people, the Yankee's mount won two of three heats, eclipsing its southern opponent.[49]

So Ellen's alter ego "William Johnson" may have accomplished more than concealing her true identity. Even if William and Ellen never intended these meanings, in a culture attuned to the triumphs and defeats of intersectional racing, the name "William Johnson"—representing a southerner, a white man, and a loser—may have registered as a send-up to the class of white American men whose opinions and economic interests justified the system of southern slavery. Fugitives like the celebrated Frederick Douglass, whose surname derived from the hero of a popular novel by Sir Walter Scott, often renamed themselves once they had arrived on northern soil, in order to mark an end to the living death of southern bondage, a new birth into freedom, and their independence and distinction from their former masters and mistresses. Ellen Craft's "William Johnson" illustrates how nomenclature could be a crucial and meaningful tool of escape as well as a commemorative ritual when the dangerous ordeal was over.

The Crafts stated in their speeches and writing that they finally made it to the North, safe in Philadelphia, on Christmas Day in 1848. They said they took about four days to make the journey: across

Georgia to Savannah's port, up the Atlantic to Charleston, following the coast again by boat to Wilmington, North Carolina, and then traveling inland through a bit of Maryland to Pennsylvania. What could have been more dramatic and moving than two members of a despised, downtrodden race gaining free soil on the very day that honored Christ, who instructed men and women to love each other in spite of their distinctions and later miraculously rose to life again from the silent tomb? Without downplaying the salutary Christian symbolism, the Crafts' 1848 arrival also connected to a secular zeitgeist that called upon the world's downtrodden men and women to unite in revolution.

In the literature of nineteenth-century abolition, the Crafts avoid close calls to make it safely from slavery to freedom. In tension with this sense of closure is also an understanding of their escape from Georgia to the free states as an initial, conditional one, one that calls upon collaboration to protect their freedom as much as it tests their own sharpness and stamina to obtain it. The contingency, hyper-vigilance, and brevity of their free months in America teaches audiences more about the bigotry, indifference, and backsliding of their contemporaries, including the abolitionists, than it speaks to any insufficiencies or lapses of their own. As their brief Boston interlude would prove, freedom for them meant oscillation between unsettled peace and danger.

CHAPTER TWO

Boston's Glorious Fugitives

> From there we went to Boston, where, thanks to William Lloyd
> Garrison, Wendell Phillips, Theodore Parker, and others, we
> lived in peace and happiness until 1850, when the fugitive slave
> law was passed.... Then it was that the Craft excitement was
> at its height. The colored people held mass meetings of protest,
> and 200 of them armed themselves and vowed that they
> would defend us until the death.
> —*Ellen Craft, quoted in "An Ex-Slave's Reminiscences"*

William and Ellen Craft's passion, inventiveness, youth, and charm,
and their love for each other and for liberty, electrified antislavery communities and transmitted currents of energy and excitement throughout transatlantic networks. Their escape had embod-
ied the melodramatic elements then so popular among mid-century
American audiences: the epic conflicts between good and evil, the
vulnerable and pretty heroine and dashingly handsome hero, the upheavals of fortune and fame, the marvelous coincidences and heavy-
handed symbolism, the nail-biting risks, the eleventh-hour rescues.
Yet their ambitions for freedom that had germinated in slavery would
nevertheless remain unrequited in the North. Uneducated descendants of enslaved Africans, they faced uncertainty about just how
long novelty, celebrity, and their enthusiasm could trump their racial genealogies and provide them opportunities to prosper and build
prosperous lives.

The omnipresent prospect of being kidnapped back into slavery
tempered their happiness at escaping it, and it demonstrated the
long reach of bondage that triumphal versions of their narrative have
glossed over in favor of the more satisfying ending represented by

their arrival to the welcoming arms of Philadelphia's and Boston's abolitionist communities. While the ongoing threat of rendition into servitude generated anxious days and sleepless nights for American fugitives like the Crafts, they risked additional treacheries: poverty, obscurity, the alienation and scorn that greeted unbidden strangers in an unwelcoming land. The money, employment, and shelter arranged by a protective, tight-knit web of antislavery friends in Boston necessitated that they return the favors, balancing personal aspirations for a family life and economic self-sufficiency with a commitment to public activism that was sincerely held and dutifully practiced, even if it frequently interrupted their own agenda as a husband and wife. Soon the Crafts were no closer to safety than they had been in the South.

By January 1849, William and Ellen had settled in Boston, the center of the American antislavery movement. They were taken under wing and mentored by numerous black and white Bostonians, including the legendary Lewis Hayden (1815–89), a magnanimous, gregarious, inspired former bondsman who hailed from Lexington, Kentucky. His prosperous household at 66 Phillips Street was a station on the Underground Railroad and, along with the African Meeting House in nearby Smith Court, a gathering place for abolitionists.[1] Hayden balanced business success with community philanthropy, but, as the historians James Oliver Horton and Lois E. Horton write in their *Black Bostonians* (1979), his efforts on behalf of the runaway slaves regularly outpaced his accomplishments in other areas. "On one occasion," they recount, "author Harriet Beecher Stowe visited his home and found thirteen fugitive slaves on the premises."[2] According to the 1850 Boston census, in his convivial, if somewhat crowded, residence, Hayden, his wife, and his children made room for the Crafts and four other unrelated black persons, very likely fugitives.[3]

On the North Slope of Beacon Hill, the denizens of Boston's free and fugitive black community who were not professionals or business owners like Hayden worked on the waterfront as ship builders and sailors, or they were employed by white families and business proprietors as domestic servants and laborers—which would be their most common source of income by 1850, or they sparred with other poor Bostonians for space and visibility on the city's thoroughfares so they could sell the crafts and wares they made and the foodstuffs that they cooked or grew. Before the Crafts arrived on the scene, fully one-fourth of black Boston's approximately two thousand residents owned their own businesses: gaming houses, barbershops, boardinghouses, and shops. Eyewitnesses and visitors to the city estimated its fugitive slave population at several hundred.[4] Gusts of wind magnified scents familiar and foreign from docked ships and teased up dresses and coattails. Gulls and swallows swooped overhead, and the occasional nor'easter slickened the pitched and arching streets. To runaways like the Crafts, such constant reminders of the fickle and protean Atlantic were connected to the idea of recapture and their sense of how far and precipitately their fortunes could plunge from security and freedom to penury and peonage.

Yet something clicked for the Crafts in Boston. Their new home augured the fruition of their long-abated dream of family warmth and stability, financial independence, and a protective Christian community. Inspired by the collective successes of Boston's African Americans, and by the individual rags-to-riches story of their benefactor Hayden, who was the purveyor of a thriving used-clothing store, William opened a "New and Second Hand" furniture and restoration business at 62 Federal Street. His establishment prospered, and he advertised it widely in the pages of *The Liberator*, the nation's largest circulating antislavery newspaper, which the inimitable William Lloyd Garrison (1805–79) published a few blocks away at 21 Cornhill.[5]

The Crafts began night school together to procure their long-delayed educations, Ellen took up sewing again to supplement William's income, and their new associate William Wells Brown acculturated them to the spectacle of the antislavery stage throughout the towns and cities of New England. Subscribing to Victorian taboos against women public speakers, William did most of the talking. Ellen politely stood, smiled, and curtsied when he ended and the audience members were ready to acknowledge her. Her performance reflected what Sarah Meer observes as the cultural prerogative in America and Great Britain that "a woman who depended on the public for her livelihood be domestic as well as commercial—that she must not be too visible despite her public position"; yet Gay Gibson Cima also maps how Ellen steps out from this domestic frame by manipulating her silent, immobile body in order to assert independence from both her husband William and from white abolitionist audiences and mentors.[6] Contemporaneous accounts of the Crafts in Boston emphasize their determination to agitate actively for an end to slavery, even as they conform to public expectations that they perform the roles of a responsible husband and breadwinner and a respectable wife and lady.[7]

In *Bound for Canaan* (2005), his history of the Underground Railroad, Fergus M. Bordewitch explains that by "portraying African Americans as bold, resourceful, and independent men and women, rather than the barely tamed savages or docile livestock that proslavery propaganda claimed," the couple's flight inspired free people on two continents to endorse the project of ending American slavery.[8] Sometime between the Crafts' arrival in Boston in early 1849 and their departure in late 1850, Ellen sought to capitalize on these themes of their story by posing in her masculine disguise for a commemorative daguerreotype, a photograph produced on a copperplate surface. She and other abolitionists recognized a new technology, the camera, and a new kind of reformer, the photographer, as tools to serve their arguments for the emancipation of African Americans in bondage. According to the art historian Deborah Willis, fifty African American daguerrotypists of the 1840s, including Jules Lion of New Orleans (1810–66), James Presley Ball of Cincinnati (1825–1904/05?), and Augustus Washington of Hartford (1820–75), owned studios in urban centers.[9]

In 1848, in addition to its stature as an antislavery center, Boston was rivaled as a photography capital only by New York City, where Mathew Brady (1822–96) kept his studio.[10] By the Civil War, which brought Brady recognition for his images of battleground carnage, mass-produced pictorial magazines and newspapers such as *Harper's Weekly* and *Frank Leslie's* circulated nationally and attracted robust readerships. They featured not only detailed illustrations and engravings but also, increasingly, photographs.[11] This daring fledgling technology was not immune to gendered and racialized politics and policies. As the historian Nell Irvin Painter has found, the best place to find photographs featuring African American men in the 1840s is police department records, not periodicals.[12]

Nevertheless, the scholars Kim Sichel and Gwendolyn DuBois Shaw confirm along with Willis that African American photographers shot dignified pictures of black community members in mid-nineteenth-century Boston. As Sichel states, "[D]aguerrotypist John B. Bailey (active in Boston during the 1840s) . . . taught James P. Ball the art of photography. . . . [Additionally,] the painter Edward Mitchell Bannister (1820–1901) was photographing in Boston in about 1840."[13] In her book *Portraits of a People: Picturing African Americans in the Nineteenth Century* (2006), Shaw invites us to consider that African American photographers working during the medium's infancy may have found precedent in "dignified, distinct, and far from stereotypical" representations of their people made by non-black artists.[14] In addition to making a livelihood, it was to effect "subversive resistance," writes Willis, to replace "negative representations" of black people in white America's literature and art with flattering, humanizing portraits, that many early African American photographers plied their trade.[15]

Frederick Douglass, who once had shared the dais with William Craft and William Wells Brown at an 1849 antislavery meeting, astutely had gauged the enormity of the photograph's influence on abolition, and of photography's influential ability to subvert southern slavery. Complaining in *The Liberator* of white artists who painted as if all black people were alike, making "the likeness of the negro, rather than of the man," Douglass himself posed for numerous photographs over his lifetime, in addition to sitting for artists who painted or sculpted his image following the current fashion.[16] Perhaps he additionally meant to imply that the new visual medium rendered in a more authentic and respectable fashion the uniqueness, beauty, and authority of individual African Americans than other artistic forms. He insisted, as Gwendolyn DuBois Shaw writes, that "until African Americans began to represent themselves they would not find artists capable or interested in portraying them with the sensitivity that the serious representation of individuals required."[17]

Ellen Craft's daguerreotype displayed her in the disguise of masculinity and whiteness that enabled her escape, yet the woman and the black underneath her garments subverted stereotypical meanings associated with her gender and race, audaciously confronting white audiences with her humanity, her intellect, and the apparent ease of her adjustment to freedom. Her decision to sit for the picture may have been inspired by Douglass, William Wells Brown, and other famed and fabulous runaways. The white male leadership of abolitionist organizations typically selected runaways whose lectures or autobiographies would verify the humanity of black people and deliver scathing indictments of the inhumanity of slavery and slaveholders. They encouraged the most compelling orators to recast their public speeches into written narratives, both to raise money for abolition and to provide themselves and their families an independent means of support.[18]

In his study *Blind Memory* (2000), Marcus Wood finds that fugitives from American slavery inserted powerful, assertive visual representations of themselves in their published memoirs, which were intended to undermine the power of conventional illustrations of them as pitiful, suffering victims.[19] Ellen Craft's direct gaze and refined masculine clothes—her change into a wealthy, albeit disabled, white man—would have shocked and threatened white British and American audiences. As the critic and scholar Teresa C. Zackodnik writes, the complexities invoked by her visual rendering—a man who was really a woman, a white man who was really a black woman, an affluent gentleman who was a pampered invalid who was really an illiterate female slave—"unsettled more than it comforted her audiences with the reassuringly familiar." This widely circulating image of a crossed-dressed Ellen Craft challenged assumptions about the fixity of gender, race, normalcy, and class that those viewing her picture may have uncritically accepted.[20]

Craft's daguerreotype survives in the form of a steel engraving reproduced opposite the title page of the first edition of *Running a Thousand Miles for Freedom* (see figure 4). In addition to mobilizing public opinion against slavery and replenishing the coffers of the antislavery cause, as William Craft implies in the preface to *Running a Thousand Miles for Freedom*, the Crafts would seek to finance the education of their growing brood of children—Charles Estlin Phillips (1852–1938), William II (born 1855), Stephen Brougham Dennoce (born 1857, known as Brougham), Alice Isabella Ellen (1866–1917, known simply as Ellen), and Alfred (born 1869)—through the sale of their 1860 narrative.[21] That they planned to enlist the engraving of Ellen in this fund-raising scheme is obvious. Years before the narrative's publication, English abolitionists advertised copies of Ellen's portrait for sale, alongside notices of *Uncle Tom* in their publications. The image of a costumed Ellen who has traversed all of those miles reflects the complex networks that supported formerly enslaved women and men as they strove to attain liberated lives. The inscriptions "After Hale's dag." and "S. A. Schoff and J. Andrews" in the bottom left and right of the engraving offer clues to a hidden history.

Instead of a black photographer, at least three white Bostonians were involved in the production of Craft's daguerreotype and the composition of the steel engraving. Hale, Schoff, and Andrews were members of the Massachusetts Charitable Mechanic Association (MCMA), an influential group of urban tradesmen. Founded in 1799, the venerable MCMA had named the patriot Paul Revere (1734 O.S.–1818) its first president, and it chiefly held educational programs for its members and competitive exhibitions of their work.[22] Luther Holman Hale (1823–?), who made the daguerreotype of Craft, occupied a studio at 109 Washington Street, near *The Liberator*'s office. Here William Craft submitted business notices for the weekly issue, and two blocks down stood the shop of bookbinder and bookseller Bela Marsh (1797–1869), who specialized in antislavery literature and regularly advertised his inventory in *The Liberator*. One block from Hale on 228 Washington Street was Stephen Alonzo Schoff (1818–1905), who engraved Craft's image and was nationally respected for the quality of his work. Joseph Andrews (1806–73), Schoff's collaborator, had toured European studios and museums in the 1840s with him, and also lived downtown, on 66 State Street.[23]

While I have not found Schoff's and Andrews's names in the membership rolls or subscription lists of local antislavery societies, other evidence, in addition to their geographical proximity to each other and the Crafts' haunts, suggests that they were sympathetic to abolition. Schoff had made an engraving of the minister Theodore Parker, who in the parlor of Lewis Hayden's house gave the Crafts the legal Christian marriage they had longed for. Andrews's work graced pages of the antislavery annual *The Liberty Bell*, edited by Maria Weston Chapman (1806–85); he illustrated books by abolitionists

ELLEN CRAFT,

The fugitive Slave.

Figure 4. Ellen Craft, the fugitive slave. Courtesy of Manuscripts, Archives, and Rare Books Division, Schomburg Center for Research in Black Culture, New York Public Library, Astor, Lenox, and Tilden Foundations..

John Greenleaf Whittier (1807–92) and Lydia Maria Child (1802–80); and he would engrave 1852 and 1853 editions of *Uncle Tom's Cabin*.

Hale's role in producing Craft's daguerreotype and engraving may suggest the paucity of black photographers in Boston during the early years of this new technology. Additionally, it was commonplace in the antebellum, urban North for African American men to find themselves barred from competing with white men like Hale, Schoff, and Andrews for employment and apprenticeship in highly skilled trades, and locked out of organizations or guilds whose members were white men. Hale, Schoff, and Andrews may have been recommended to the Crafts by antislavery friends. Whether the Crafts approached them on their own initiative to market Ellen's story, or whether they had been encouraged to do so by Hayden, William Wells Brown, Parker, or other New England abolitionists they had met, is uncertain. It is difficult to determine the extent of the Crafts' agency and decision making in this process.

Perhaps what is knowable is that the couple maneuvered between the good intentions of northern abolitionists to point them down safe and remunerative paths and their own willfulness and determination to chart their own direction in life. Ellen and William may no longer have been required to jump at the Collinses' commands, but in the precariousness of nominal northern freedom they turned to white as well as black Bostonians and activists to give them a leg up financially until they could stand on their own. These allies helped groom them as writers and public speakers, managed their appearances in the antislavery press, and helped protect them from kidnappers and other harm. The cultural historian Ann Fabian reminds us that "stories told by former slaves did not always end with the narrators' incorporation into a free society; they ended with narrators on the lecture circuit—no longer enslaved, but suspended somewhere between slavery and freedom."[24] On the other hand, as Zackodnik cautions, it is important to temper interpretations of how an ex-slave woman like Craft may have been victimized and commodified, by the activists and audiences who eagerly sought her story, with the evidence that she and other fugitives did actively exercise "agency or choice" in decisions regarding how their bodies and writing would gain them attention, earn them a living, provide them with a degree of security and safety, and relieve them to a degree from being haunted by threats of kidnapping and re-enslavement.[25]

Transatlantic antislavery writers also latched on to both the populist appeal and commercial possibilities of a good retelling of the Crafts' escape. This occurred at the very moment when theatrical productions catering to the tastes of white working-class and middle-class Americans and Britons made African American dignity a struggle and roles sometimes difficult to swallow.[26] *Uncle Tom* plays based on the famous novel, often rather loosely, were produced by antislavery and proslavery camps on both sides of the Atlantic in the early 1850s. The flagrant disregard of authorial intention and ownership that characterized such productions spurred Stowe to pen her own dramatization, *The Christian Slave* (1855). In a pointed lesson to imitators, she then granted the black elocutionist Mary E. Webb (1829–59) her official permission to read it before enraptured American and British audiences.[27] Three years later, the rift between proslavery and antislavery factions had heightened, and the prospect of a full-blown civil war loomed large. At this time another widely known antislavery writer, Lydia Maria Child, turned her time and talents to theatrical performance, rehearsing the Crafts' escape.

Child had always craved knowledge. In an era when it was thought possible to overeducate middle-class girls, public opinion could brand a white woman like her a freak, making her an outcast. Many people believed that too much education for girls would render them unfit for the practical skills and self-sacrificing natures expected of suitable wives and mothers. Yet she had seized upon the books in her father's massive library and a steady supply from an older brother at Harvard, and in adulthood she combined this thirst for learning with incisive writing skill and an unrelenting commitment to stamping out social injustices. The editor of the *National Anti-Slavery Standard* (1840–70) for two years, she came to abolition with a wide-ranging résumé. Not only had she authored publications for children, novels, domestic manuals, and articles for periodicals, she had a husband and family that looked to her for a steady and constant stream of income. Her interactions with fugitive American slaves ranged from providing editorial suggestions for Harriet Jacobs's pre-Civil War narrative to negotiating after the war with the influential Boston publishing house Ticknor and Fields to produce a reader called *The Freedmen's Book* (1868).[28]

Child's *The Stars and Stripes: A Melo-Drama* (1855) appeared in *The Liberty Bell*, a book edited by the abolitionist Maria Weston Chapman (1806–85) and sold annually at fund-raisers and bazaars on behalf of the American Anti-Slavery Society. Like William Wells Brown's autobiographical five-act drama *The Escape; or, A Leap for Freedom* (1858), which he later permitted to be performed publicly after writing it without "the remotest thought that it would ever be seen by the public eye,"[29] Child may have intended her play as a closet drama to be read privately instead of performed publicly, to remain within a community of activists in America and Great Britain who would have read and bought and copied from *The Liberty Bell*.[30] Like Woodson's article about the Crafts to come in the next century, Child's dramatization underscores how writers reimagined the Crafts' story and straightened its crooked borders to make it fit cultural expectations about slavery and freedom, gender and race.

Child imagines William as a "genteel-looking light mulatto," proud and sensitive, his image calling forth the epic heroic metonyms of flashing eye, clenching fist, and swelling breast. He chafes under the humiliations of slavery and the deferential posture that it compels him to occupy. She presents Ellen, "who might pass for a white woman," as a compliant, ornamental wife who adds joy to their "humble little apartment" by singing beautifully. She trills snatches of opera that she has heard in the big house instead of the spirituals favored by field hands, and she warbles like a bobolink, a songbird whose white and yellow feathers appear to cloak its black ones.[31]

Child erases the public story that the Crafts told about running away for the sake of their unborn children. Instead she presents the imminence of Ellen's rape by her master and William's inability to protect her as the catalysts for their escape. Like the embellishments of Theodore Parker and James Freeman Clarke, Child invents a narrative for the silences surrounding Ellen's body. In the third scene of her play, Ellen confesses to William, "I have been afraid to tell you all my troubles, for fear you would do something rash, and then they would burn you.... But now massa has gone away, and you will have time to get cool before he comes back; and so I will tell you all. When I am at the big house, sewing for missis, as sure as she goes out to ride, he comes into my room and asks me to sing, and tells me how pretty I am. And—and—I know by his ways that he don't mean any good. He gave me this breast-pin, and I was afraid not to take it."[32] This confession shares more in common with what audiences knew of Ellen's mother Maria than Ellen herself, based on what she and William publicly related. Ellen's singing in this scene, an ostensibly miniscule way in which a free and respectable woman makes a house a home, becomes amplified into a thinly veiled symbol of how constantly rape was a threat, of how easily masters and overseers could distort a casual gesture or innocent word into an invitation for abuse, of how they did not even have to justify their assaults. In slavery, real or imagined, no amount of courage or bravery that William might muster could save Ellen.

To make it north, Child leads the Crafts through a thicket of Christian and classical symbolism. They hide on a "swampy island in the middle of a dense forest," replete with "wolves and snakes," which stands for the nefarious motives and never-ending mendacity of slaveholders. They travel on a "night-journey" under cover of "the darkest of the shadows," which conflates bondage in body and spirit with the Twenty-Third Psalm's "shadow of the valley of death." They drag themselves to the northern border of the southern states to discover an "open country" bisected by a "broad river," which alludes to Canaan and the Jordan River. Black Christians believed their souls crossed over from the hell of slavery to the heaven of the afterlife, and in Child's play they cross from the fetters of slavery to the freedom of the northern states or Canada. Here at the river they meet a Charon-like boatman, a runaway slave named Dick, who ferries them, interred temporarily in barrels, to the opposite shore and to rejuvenating freedom.[33]

For all of its fast-paced, rollicking action, Child's play seems amazingly blasé about Ellen's disguise as a southern white planter. William broaches the subject of escape, entreating, "Dear Ellen, if you love me, try to be courageous. I know where there is a suit of young massa's clothes, and I have no doubt they will fit you. You can pass for a white lad, and I can be your servant." Taking the initiative, he volunteers to "go and bring young massa's clothes" and he advises Ellen to begin "thinking how to pass for a white young gentleman, if anybody speaks to us."[34] That's it for the discussion of her disguise. Out of the eight scenes that comprise *Stars and Stripes*, only one would have exposed viewing audiences to Ellen costumed in male clothes. Child leaves no room for Ellen's male garments to convey the myriad meanings of race, class, disability, and gender that literary critics, historians, and experts in popular culture have assigned to her masculine attire. Nor does she linger on the daringly public route by rail, carriage, and steamer that the Crafts took to the northern states. Instead she depicts how members of the Underground Railroad, white and black, southern and northern, male and female, assist the Crafts and other fugitives in escaping to Canadian shores.

Child seems to minimize the gender-bending sensationalism of Ellen's disguise, and she involves the interracial, collaborative Underground Railroad more consistently and strongly in their flight to freedom. Bypassing Philadelphia and Boston, she sends the Crafts to Canada. Such changes from fact help to underscore the well-timed themes of patriotism and union in *The Stars and Stripes*. In actuality the Crafts spent the Civil War years—and nearly two decades of their life together—in England, but Child has it otherwise. Child transplants the Crafts in her play to South Carolina, which would become the first of southern states to secede, with the rebel salvos on Fort Sumter rumbling in 1861. Celebrating the Fourth of July, an inebriated group of slaveholders ironically closes the final verse of Robert Treat Paine's "Adams and Liberty," an ode from the American Revolution, with the refrain that "Ne-er shall the sons of Columbia be slaves!" Enter the US flag, symbol of the hard-won liberty they sing about, crowned by a tricolored French liberty cap, handled by enslaved African Americans who are "attended by a vulgar-looking overseer, somewhat intoxicated."[35] William sees this farce for the mockery of patriotism it is, and he recites to Ellen the verses:

> Oppression should not linger
> Where starry banners wave;
> The swelling about of Freedom
> Should echo for the slave.[36]

Abolitionist writers, like Child in this case, often pointed to the national flag not as a symbol of freedom but as evidence of how Americans had foreclosed genuine patriotism and true republicanism in favor of an institution that rewarded greed and corruption.[37] They evoked the flag's stripes as a double entendre that alluded to the effects of the overseer's lash. They shamed the nation with the accusation that it was now more oppressive than England, and like the abolitionist characters in Child's play they held August 1 celebrations in honor of the day Britain officially emancipated the West Indian slaves. As they debuted in American antislavery forums during 1849 and 1850 and charmed the New England abolitionists they encountered, the real William and Ellen Craft learned how much power lay in such thoughtful critiques of Americans who supported slavery and thus made a lie of their country's founding principles of equality and liberty. Child's *The Stars and Stripes* ends with Canadians welcoming William and Ellen Craft with a rousing "God save the Queen!"[38] Likewise, the real Crafts would preface their 1860 memoir with an epigraph from the eighteenth-century British abolitionist William Cowper (1731–1800):

Slaves cannot breathe in England: if their lungs
Receive our air, that moment they are free;
They touch our country, and their shackles fall."[39]

At the start of their escape in *The Stars and Stripes*, William remarks to Ellen that they "got along very well, thanks to your white face, and passing yourself for a slaveholder." After a long night's journey, he changes his mind. "Your clothes are so worn and dusty," he says, "that you can hardly pass for the son of a rich slaveholder; but you may be taken for a poor white, emigrating with his only nigger." Just as Ellen exchanges one class for another, both Crafts enact a racial passing when, to get to Canada, they blacken their white-looking faces in order to blend in with a group of African American mourners. They blur distinctions again at an antislavery picnic where William "has a neat new dress, and wears a brown wig," and Ellen dons a veil among a group of veiled white women so she "need not be easily recognized."[40] By associating William and Ellen with the ability to transgress categories of class, race, gender, and region, Child can situate the couple's escape squarely within the play's themes of equality and liberty. Further, she can imply how the patriarchal institution of slavery oppresses more groups than the slaves—poor white men, free black Americans, and middle-class white women, to name but three.

At midcentury, Child would not be the only antislavery writer to fictionalize the Crafts' escape. In *Uncle Tom's Cabin*, Stowe's near-white heroine Eliza alludes to Ellen Craft when she disguises herself as a man and her son Harry as a little girl to cross the Canadian border undetected.[41] In *The Bondwoman's Narrative* by ex-slave Hannah Bond (born ca. 1830s), one of the earliest novels by an African American woman writer, a girl named Ellen dresses in a boy's clothing in order to slip out of bondage.[42] William Wells Brown sketches the story of his friends the Crafts in his novel *Clotel* (1853), and he commissioned the painting of a panel depicting Ellen in her disguise for his traveling panorama in England.[43]

As 1850 unfolded in Boston, William and Ellen Craft desired to follow the literary examples of Brown and other antislavery authors, and they considered writing a book in order to assist the cause and to gain a more independent financial footing—to help wean themselves from economic reliance on Boston's antislavery community. Yet their narrative would not appear until a decade later, during which time a more pressing challenge intervened. On September 18, 1850, President Millard Fillmore (1800–74) signed into law a section of the Compromise of 1850 intended to appease the nation's restive proslavery faction. The treacherous Fugitive Slave Law pressed runaway communities and families to the ropes, as implied by the urgent tone of posters warning of kidnappers (see figure 5). This legislation entitled all slave-owners to obtain federal assistance to recapture their "property" that had escaped to the free states. It obligated federal judges, commissioners, and other authorities to marshal their resources and extend aid to any southerners who wished to recommit their wayward slaves to manacles and chains. It punished abolitionist sympathizers who harbored fugitives—or who stubbornly refused to help identify them or track down them down—with exorbitant fines "not exceeding one thousand dollars" and prison sentences of up to six months. It tacked on additional fines of one thousand dollars for every slave who got away. The federal commissioners who oversaw such efforts could

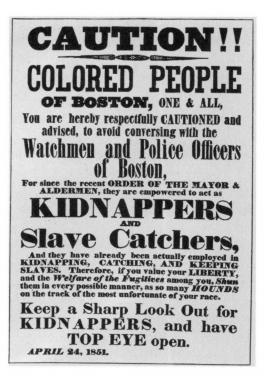

Figure 5. An 1851 poster warning blacks in Boston about slave catchers. Courtesy Photographs and Prints Division, Schomburg Center for Research in Black Culture, New York Public Library, Astor, Lenox, and Tilden Foundations.

earn as much as ten dollars a head for the people they reclaimed.[44] In their memoir *Running a Thousand Miles for Freedom*, published one decade after the Fugitive Slave Law of 1850, the Crafts would blame this odious legislation on the arsenic climate created by "unprincipled and tyrannical Yankees," "the low Yankee prejudice," and "mean Yankee excuses."[45] Yet they balanced these excoriations with a mitigating factor: their own vision of interracial and geographical unity, where ties of affiliation and mutuality united fugitives like them to "very kind and hospitable friends, both in America and England."[46]

Former slaves who had taken refuge in the North packed their bags and headed for the greater security of Canada or England, and the Crafts became the quarry in a three-week-long cat-and-mouse chase. In late October 1850, seeking to make a national example of them, Collins paid two bounty hunters, the Macon jailer Willis H.

Hughes and John Knight, a cabinetmaker who had worked in the same shop as William, to recapture the couple and return them to Georgia. Abolitionists mobilized to thwart the couple's recapture. A biracial group of activists, the Boston Vigilance Committee had formed in 1846 and included the Crafts' friends Hayden, Parker, and Clarke, as well as such prominent African Americans as the attorney Robert Morris (1823–82) and the abolitionist and historian William Cooper Nell (1816–74). They devised a strategy consisting of constant harassment and shakedowns of the scruffy, rough-edged mercenaries: pelting them with eggs and rotten food, arresting them for driving their carriages recklessly through the streets, detaining them for smoking in public. James Oliver Horton and Lois Horton observe that middle-class African American women also assisted in the Vigilance Committee's efforts, although, since committee records "identify these women only in relation to male family heads," the details of their involvement are murky and difficult to discern. Southern and northern papers and the British antislavery press gave extensive coverage to the committee's defiance of the Fugitive Slave Law, and to Hughes and Knight's rebuffed attempts to arrest the Crafts.[47]

The Vigilance Committee coordinated hiding places for the Crafts. Its members divided the celebrity pair and, like the pieces on a checkerboard, moved them from safe house to safe house in Boston and its suburbs of Brookline and Cambridge, and to the northern Massachusetts port town of Marblehead. Lewis Hayden sheltered William at 66 Phillips Street, and, brandishing a match over two kegs of gunpowder, he vowed to blow his home and the slave catchers attempting to trespass it straight to kingdom come before he surrendered his friend to them. As tensions between the committee and Hughes and Knight heated up, Ellen was also sequestered alone—at the Brookline residence of antislavery lawyer Ellis Gray Loring (1803–58) and with the Underground Railroad conductor William Ingersoll Bowditch (1819–1909) and his family at 9 Toxteth Street in Brookline.[48]

Ellen also lay low one week at the 1 Exeter Place home of Reverend Parker, so close to the Beacon Hill neighborhood where she and William had once lived unmolested. Parker was a fortunate talisman. With the good reverend officiating, a pistol in hand just in case they were discovered, the Crafts reunited in Lewis Hayden's home on November 7, 1850, to take formal marriage vows in the Christian ceremony that for so long had been their dream.[49] The Boston marriage registry for 1850, which I examined in the Massachusetts Archives, records their signatures.

The page that officially documents the Crafts' 1850 union (in what would become a frequent error over the centuries, their surname is misspelled "Crafts") presents an unsentimental inventory of information, typical of such public records over the centuries. Entered in columns that march across the page are the date of their marriage, their names, their residence and ages, the groom's occupation, the place of their births and the names of their parents, that this was their first marriage, and who married them. Decoding the incomplete and scattershot archives of African American people like the Crafts necessitates, as Lois Brown has stated, an ear placed to the ground for the "riotous, symphonic, insistent national, international, pan-African noise" that rumbles beneath the orderly appearance of such texts.[50]

Among over a dozen listings of Boston marriages in November and December, the Crafts are the only couple on the page whose parents' first names are omitted. Most of the couples hailed from Boston and other New England or Middle Atlantic places—Dedham and Braintree, Massachusetts; Philadelphia, Pennsylvania; Rhode Island and Maryland. A few hint at stories of Irish and Scottish immigrants to whom the industrializing North had promised warm shelter and full bellies if they were willing to spin, weave, stand, and sew long hours in the factories and mills, heft heavy bales of merchandise as dock laborers, sail the seas as mariners, or sacrifice family and personal relationships to earn wages as live-in tutors and domestics in more prosperous households.[51] In contrast, the Crafts' southern place of origination bears silent testimony to a different story altogether. From their ancestors kidnapped from the African continent or transported from the Caribbean during the transatlantic slave trade, to the forcible separations from family and friends they have witnessed and endured in plantation slavery, to the most recent disruption of their lives and their union as Hughes and Knight pursued them, the Crafts' Georgia birthplace suggests how slavery's impact distinguished the prospects of African American fugitives from those of other groups hoping to abandon wretched conditions for security, freedom, and justice on America's shores.

At least the Crafts could say that they finally had exchanged the sacred vows they had longed for during their courtship, even as they were spirited out of Boston by the Underground Railroad. Like the cramped attic space where the fugitive slave Harriet Ann Jacobs lay hidden for seven years and far predating the secret domicile of the young Anne Frank (1929–45) in the Nazi-occupied Netherlands, the Crafts lay concealed in a tiny hiding space. They huddled in a room constructed under the floorboards at 236 Washington Street in the Marblehead, Essex County, home of Betsy Dodge (born ca. 1815) and her husband Simeon (born ca. 1819), a carpenter and an Underground Railroad conductor.[52]

The Vigilance Committee's insurgent tactics worked. They set a dazed Hughes and Knight into a tailspin, and the two defeated agents of Dr. Collins abandoned their mission. However, this did little to inspire a victory celebration by the Crafts and by those who had protected them. Exhausted, the couple longed to recover some permanence and peace after the chase that had imperiled them for weeks. So they struck out on another icy winter flight like the one-thousand-mile escape they had made almost two years earlier. This time they traveled secretly to Halifax, Nova Scotia, once Boston abolitionists gave them the all-clear.

The city of Halifax, Nova Scotia, which started as a military fortification and port for British troops and munitions, often is shown in a lesser light than the vibrant communities of American fugitives in the Canadian West, where the flames of abolition, temperance, and other social movements were kept burning by leaders such as Mary Ann Shadd (1823–93) and Samuel Ringgold Ward (1817–ca. 1866), who co-edited Toronto's *The Provincial Freeman*; Henry Bibb (1815–1854), who founded *The Voice of the Fugitive* in Sandwich, now Windsor, Ontario; and Josiah Henson (1789–1883), who was the real-life inspiration for Harriet Beecher Stowe's character Uncle Tom.[53] Halifax's history as a safe haven for African Americans from the American Revolution to the War of 1812 has been foregrounded in national histories and exhibits of African Nova Scotia. By strategically de-emphasizing

Underground Railroad connections to Atlantic Canada, in favor of their involvement in these larger migrations, African Nova Scotians may have gained more visibility and importance in Canada's multi-ethnic national narrative.

Bridglal Pachai and Henry Bishop observe that Halifax and more broadly all of Nova Scotia attracted American fugitives up and down the Eastern Seaboard in part because of the area's shorter run of slavery. Compared to longer spans in some New England states and the American South, slavery had ended in Halifax in 1808, due to harsh weather conditions and inhospitable soil that impeded the development of a plantation economy, as well as local courts that obstructed it. As the War for Independence concluded and through the early 1780s, over three thousand free blacks and formerly enslaved Africans, Black Loyalists who had allied with the British, fled reprisals or re-enslavement for offers of the Crown's protection in Nova Scotia and neighboring New Brunswick. During and after the War of 1812, between 1813 and 1816, another wave of over two thousand African Americans settled in Halifax and surrounding communities. This second large diaspora, collectively dubbed "the Black Refugees," established segregated towns around Halifax, such as "Preston, Hammonds Plains, Beech Hill, Cobequid Road, Windsor Road, Africville, Birchtown, Digby, and Guysborough."[54] In the twenty-first century, many of these historic communities founded by Black Refugees have disappeared in the wake of efforts to push them off their land. This is disturbingly similar to how Gullah and Geechee communities have lost ground to wealthy real estate and tourism interests that have constructed exclusive homes and resorts on the Sea Islands, precipitating increases in property taxes that force black families off the land who have resided there for generations.[55]

The Crafts lodged in Halifax with a Canadian minister and his family, whose hospitality demonstrated how religious institutions in the African Nova Scotian community maintained nimble and robust abolitionist networks in eastern Canada.[56] Richard Preston's Cornwallis Street African Baptist Church was a hive of such activism, supported by Haligonian mutual aid and benevolent associations that proudly announced themselves and suggested channels of assistance to the fugitives from the South like William and Ellen.[57] The Crafts booked passage during the final week of November 1850 on the SS *Cambria*, a British royal mail steamship captained by John Leitch. Constructed for the wealthy Cunard company in late 1844, the *Cambria*, and later its sister ship the SS *Hibernia*, quickly earned reputations as the fastest steam vessels plying the transatlantic mail and passenger route between coastal Massachusetts and Great Britain, skimming the distance as fast as "nine days, twenty hours, thirty minutes out to Boston and eight days, twenty-two hours, forty-four minutes back to Liverpool, reaching an average speed of almost twelve knots."[58]

Samuel Cunard's scrappy firm boasted an impeccable reputation for reliable adherence to its timetable and "austere" comfort in the decor of its cabins.[59] Yet the latter characteristic would bear out as a discomforting irony for the Crafts and other fugitives from American slavery like them. Five years earlier on the *Cambria*'s run from Boston to Liverpool, Frederick Douglass had famously been booked in a berth in steerage. The company feared that its passengers "would object to such social intimacy across races." On his return voyage to America two years later, a Liverpudlian agent for Cunard sold Douglass a cabin room only on the condition that he take it "by himself, eat his meals alone, and not mingle with saloon passengers."[60] The Crafts themselves were twice rebuffed when they visited the Cunard office in Halifax. The ticket agents attempted to mislead them with advice that they would have to wait until the ship's arrival before purchasing their passage, or that by the time it did reach Halifax from its Boston port of departure, the steamer would already "come full."[61]

On December 11, 1850, the *Cambria* with its extraordinary passengers completed the Atlantic crossing and dropped anchor in Liverpool.[62] To insure their immediate financial and social survival, they had to contemplate surrendering themselves to the mercies of British abolitionist organizations and other like-minded reform groups.[63] Yet hope continued to beckon. They had come this far together, and together they would prepare to greet or grapple with what befell them.

CHAPTER THREE

Running a Thousand Miles in England

[A]s the free air of good old England agrees so well with
my wife and our dear little ones, as well as with myself, it
is not at all likely we shall return at present to the "peculiar
institution" of chains and stripes.
—*William Craft, in* Running a Thousand Miles for Freedom

The Crafts disembarked from the *Cambria* to a brittle and blustery midwinter Liverpool. Over six years before, Frederick Douglass had sailed the same ship, stepped down onto the same docks, and then charmed the British public and won converts to antislavery with his polished manners, magnetic gaze, thundering oratory, and riveting narrative.[1] The Crafts would eventually produce in England a memoir of their years in slavery and brief, nominal freedom in North America. Their book would invite transatlantic audiences to consider the ways in which justifications for slavery dishonored their humanity, disinherited their race, and destroyed their familial and community bonds. In the memoir the Crafts represent themselves and their allies with a focus on collaboration, liberation, and brotherhood and sisterhood, defying the institution that threatened to sever these alliances and their benefits.

As antislavery activists in England, the Crafts would work to debunk misleading public perceptions that imagined the South full of "pleasant homes" with kind and gentle masters and mistresses and obedient and faithful servants.[2] By demonstrating how this paradisiacal vision of slavery masked the institution's genuine horrors, their memoir would extend this discussion.[3] It would also insist upon supplanting this false and mythic dream of slavery's harmonious households with the construction and recoveries of new dreams that "gesture continually," as John Ernest writes, "toward the tantalizing promise of domestic security."[4] The narrative's publication in England points to its potential appeal to British audiences as a self-improvement narrative that would intersect with other national discussions, about such topics as pauperism and temperance. Additionally, *Running a Thousand Miles for Freedom* tempers its vision of a harmonious marriage and family for formerly enslaved persons like the Crafts by lacing such relationships with violence both during and after slavery. It does this even as it presents the transatlantic abolition movement as an alternative community and metaphorical family that offers protection and succor in the face of such violence.

As the Crafts disembarked from the *Cambria*, they would have heard British, African, and Caribbean accents rising and falling around them, and they must have felt both apprehension and hope. Colds had consigned them to bed in Halifax, delaying their purchase of tickets for an overseas passage and increasing the tensions surrounding their escape. During their rough crossing of the Atlantic finally, as ticketed passengers, Ellen had struggled with respiratory problems, "and was also so ill that [William] did not believe she could live to see Liverpool."[5]

A long, bloody history of traffic in bodies had yielded Liverpool its riches. From the middle to late eighteenth century, numerous European ships involved in the transatlantic slave trade—from western Africa to the Americas to England, then back to Africa again—had listed their port of origin as Liverpool.[6] Yet England had legally ended the slave trade in 1807 and slavery throughout the British Empire in 1833, and the Crafts' disembarkation point stood as a powerful metonym for that country. America had fallen short of the values it had pledged to uphold, but England, for all its other arcane traditions, seemed ahead of the game. As they would remark in *Running a Thousand Miles for Freedom*, England represented to them "a truly free and glorious country; where no tyrant ... dare come and lay violent hands upon us."[7]

Other published recollections by former slaves, such as the *Life of William Grimes, the Runaway Slave* (1825), the first known book-length American slave narrative, and *Twice Sold, Twice Ransomed,* the 1926 autobiography of Mr. and Mrs. L. P. and Emma Ray, have addressed the ways in which human property who looked white, like Ellen Craft, challenged justifications for American slavery and scrambled assumptions about respectability and authority.[8] Yet *Running a Thousand Miles for Freedom* is no boilerplate slave's story and resists easy comparisons to other printed texts in this genre. For example, the classic nineteenth-century slave narrative enshrines the story of a solitary man surmounting Sisyphean obstacles in order to assert his humanity and virtue. These texts are written examples of what the scholar Gerald L. Early has named as "the black American meta-narrative of heroic or noble victimization," where an African American strives against institutionalized racism and social and political oppression in order to claim an equal place at democracy's table.[9] In the typical slave narrative, it is business as usual for a masculine hero to engage in this epic struggle, and considerably fewer numbers of them were written or related by women or featured female protagonists.

Only "12 percent of the known published narratives" were written by women, Frances Smith Foster states in her *Witnessing Slavery* (1994), and the vast majority of these did not consist of single-authored, separately published texts.[10] The demands that slavery made on motherhood, and the labor divisions and assignments that confined them mostly to domestic duties and field labor, meant that enslaved women were less mobile than men. Writes Deborah Gray White, "It was female bondage, more than male bondage, that meant being tied to the immediate environment of plantation and farm."[11] Enslaved African American men who made it to freedom were positioned to benefit from speaking tours, where they could practice weaving riveting oral narratives of slavery and test the persuasiveness of their antislavery arguments before writing or dictating their experiences. Those men who did escape to the North successfully, and who were anointed by virtue of their confidence and charisma to share stories of their travails in bondage at antislavery lectures and meetings, entered a public world where, as Philip Gould observes, oratory "was a largely masculine mode of expression."[12]

As a man and woman escaping together, and as an attractive, forceful pair who spoke and wrote together against the bondage they had escaped, the Crafts invite us to consider how their story emphasizes connection, collaboration, and partnership. Following their admission of privilege, the Crafts say that they did suffer the legal disenfranchisement shared with all men and women in slavery, including "above all, the fact that another man had the power to tear from our cradle the new-born babe and sell it in the shambles like a brute, and then scourge us if we dared to lift a finger to save it from such a fate." The "poisonous dagger of separation" from their loved ones, due to greedy transactions that devalued and disregarded their love, was the martyrdom they most feared.[13]

The publication history of *Running a Thousand Miles for Freedom* is intertwined with the Crafts' personal project of restoring security and family stability in their lives. As evidence, their memoir gives just a passing glance to the "incessant cruelty" of Ellen's first mistress during her infancy and childhood and instead pauses to linger on Ellen's separation "from her mother, and also from several other dear friends." William assigns his first master "the reputation of being a very humane and Christian man," only to admit that this man "thought nothing of selling my poor old father, and dear aged mother, at separate times, to different persons," followed shortly thereafter by his sister and brother who had been spared from the first round of auctions.[14] Through accounts of the kidnapping of the German immigrant Salomé Müller (born ca. 1809) into slavery, the seizure and sale of beautiful black women into sexual concubinage, and Ellen's mixed-race genealogy, the Crafts implicate slave owners' hypocrisies about racial purity and mixing.[15]

William Craft intended the memoir to raise funds in support of the antislavery movement. Yet it is also probable that, like the formerly enslaved Louisa Picquet (born 1828) who raised money among northern subscribers in "the fond hope of yet meeting her long-lost mother once more in this world," he counted on the revenues from the book's sales to assist in rediscovering and reuniting with scattered family members.[16] "[P]artly by lecturing occasionally, and through the sale of an engraving of [Ellen] in the disguise in which she escaped, together with the extreme kindness and generosity of . . . friends," he worked assiduously to raise funds that would "restore" his enslaved sister, who had been located in a household in Mississippi, to the arms of his now-free mother.[17]

As early as 1857, William had been publicly seeking donations to emancipate his sister.[18] At the time of the publication of the Crafts' memoir he admits to having "nearly accomplished" the goal of buying this sibling out of slavery, which suggests that at least a portion of the sales would be dedicated toward securing her freedom.[19] The first-hand knowledge that he and Ellen possessed of slavery's indignities, including the knowledge that his sister would be vulnerable to sexual victimization—"the most infamous purposes," as it is delicately put in the narrative, that enslaved women risked at the whims of "licentious monsters"—must have brought some urgency to the task of completing the book.[20] Nine years after he and Ellen arrived in England, during which time the couple had juggled fund-raising with the business of supporting their growing family, William's sense of urgency about publishing the memoir may explain, one reviewer noted, why it is thin on original material and "does not contain any facts which had not already been published in another form."[21] Since William wanted to hasten the book's completion so as to fund the manumission of his sister, he may have welcomed and even solicited the sections of the narrative that Geoffrey Sanborn has identified as having been written by William Wells Brown, the Crafts' friend and mentor.[22]

Similarly, we know that after the Civil War, Ellen Craft posted inquiries from overseas to American antislavery activists, hoping to locate her mother, Maria Smith, among the freedpeople. In 1865, American and British friends assisted the Crafts in locating Ellen's mother "after fifty-seven years spent in slavery." In England, "Miss Lushington sought the assistance of J. W. Probyn, Esq., of the Reform Club, and that gentleman, . . . applied to Dr. Fred Tomkins, of Lincoln's Inn, in order to obtain his assistance." In the United States, "through the assistance of numerous friends," including the old abolitionist lawyer Wendell Phillips, "a communication" was made with a Union general that determined that Smith was "alive and well" in Macon. "Funds were sent" to the abolitionist Levi Coffin of Cincinnati, who, "with Frances Shaw, Esq., and the Rev. W. Hawkins, M. A., of New York," finalized arrangements for Smith's "transit . . . to London." The *Newcastle Courant* painted a picture of "a trembling pale-faced ladylike" Ellen Craft, a darker son by her side, greeting "that parent so dear to them, who seemed like one risen from the dead."[23]

In October 1865, five years after *Running a Thousand Miles for Freedom* had been circulating among British and American readers and after it had gone into two editions (1860 and 1861), Ellen and her mother were reunited in England.[24] Such were the personal dramas that had given urgency to writing *Running a Thousand Miles for Freedom* and insuring its success. Published outside of the United States on the eve of the Civil War, the Crafts' narrative also can be understood as a print production that participates in the seemingly impossible project of reuniting families lost in slavery and in war that, according the historian Heather Andrea Williams, galvanized formerly enslaved communities after Emancipation Day. Using resources from the government, private organizations funded by white Americans, and a burgeoning network of African American churches and schools and regional and national periodicals, as well as relying on "centuries of collective experience developing resources out of what seemed like nothing," ex-slaves like the Crafts stopped at almost nothing to knit together their families severed by the auction block.[25]

British spellings in the book indicate consideration of its English audience, as do descriptions of "American railway carriages" that are "constructed differently to those in England," but references to Queen Elizabeth I and other historical figures and events from Britain's past register like the voice of a native addressing a tourist.[26] *Running a Thousand Miles for Freedom* was advertised in periodicals such as *The Anti-Slavery Advocate*, also published, incidentally, for the Anglo-American Antislavery Society by the Crafts' editor William Tweedie (1821–74). A Quaker and a temperance man, Tweedie, who also would famously bring out Harriet Jacobs's *Incidents in the Life of a Slave Girl* in England as *The Deeper Wrong* (1862), advertised the Crafts' 1860 memoir among such practical titles as *Harry Birket: The Story of a Man Who Helped Himself* and *The Struggles of a Village Lad; or, There is Nothing Like Trying*.[27] This points to what Eric Gardner has observed, that didactic books with a variety of messages were then published, with abolitionism but one of many, and the slave narratives were not necessarily marketed first and foremost as antiracist or antislavery texts to transatlantic nineteenth-century readers.[28] This suggests that accounts of the Crafts' self-sufficiency were meant to find a sympathetic reception among parents, ministers, teachers, and other adults bent on instructing British children on the virtues of sacrifice, piety, prayer, and hard work. The inclusion of the Crafts' *Running a Thousand Miles for Freedom* in booklists where self-improvement themes were dominant undermined slavery's nonsensical assumptions about the alterity and inferiority of black Africans and the dominance and supremacy of white Europeans.

"It is true," the Crafts confide in the first paragraph of their 1860 narrative, "our condition as slaves was not by any means the worst."[29] Certainly, when compared to those of other African Americans such as their colleague Frederick Douglass, their experiences in slavery seemed milder. His torments had run the gamut from "the great pleasure in whipping a slave" that characterized his first master's overseer, Mr. Plummer, to the "cursing, raving, cutting, and slashing" of the aptly named overseer Mr. Severe and the overseer Gore's "savage barbarity."[30] In his 1848 memoir William Wells Brown observed that in even the "mild" atmosphere of Missouri slavery, as a privileged young house servant "better fed, better clothed, and not obliged to rise at the ringing of the bell," he had "often laid and heard the crack of the whip, and the screams of the slave," and soon enough himself become the target of slaveholders' violent meltdowns.[31] Harriet Jacobs (ca. 1813–97) too overwhelmed her brief reminiscences of "six years of happy childhood" with a lengthier saga of the following domestic abuse and sexual overtures that cascaded down on her through adolescence and motherhood while she remained within the cruel Flint family.[32]

Slavery denied the freedom and humanity of every enslaved person, and it traumatized every slave with its arbitrariness, instability, and irrationality, and with its evilness and persistent threats of violence. Therefore, the Crafts' acknowledgement of holding a privileged status in the slave community, like Brown's and Jacobs's qualified descriptions of milder or softer experiences of slavery, inevitably remind free readers of the contingency and irony of such transitory positions of safety or ease. Within a transatlantic antislavery project that, as Gould writes, had made "exposing the evils of the Southern plantation (and the false paternalistic myths supporting it)" its "central" fixation, the Crafts' concession that their story deviates from more harrowing descriptions of slavery may have everything to do with inspiring trust in the veracity of their story.[33] By positioning themselves as ones who have not suffered "the worst" in slavery, as a prelude to describing how they escaped it, the Crafts invite readers to consider how many more enslaved persons resent their captivity and attempt to surmount even greater obstacles than those they confronted. They establish a tone of truth telling and authenticity that will strengthen their repeated objections in the narrative to fallacious arguments that slavery is benevolent and that slaves are the lucky beneficiaries of merciful slaveholders.

While their memoir circles back regularly to their commitment to establish a happy marriage in freedom, William and Ellen Craft equally imply the menace that slavery poses to such a sacred union by associating it with implied or actual violence. After all, as an extreme example, their own nuptials had taken place in the context of slave catchers lurking nearby to abscond with them at any moment, a friend ready to blow his house down rather than see them remanded to bondage, and a minister arming the groom for a possible shootout even as he blessed the couple and bade them go forth into a peaceful future. As Tess Chakkalakal and Frances Smith Foster have examined in their scholarship on literary treatments of African American family and romance, marriage and commitment were viewed by African American readers and writers as running the gamut from blissfully companionate to pragmatically businesslike, and the idea that happy marriages were foundational for the collective advancement of the race carried cachet even before emancipation.[34] Yet such associations that took their cue from discursive streams and popular culture in the wider society were inflected by the realities of racial and social violence that affected both enslaved and free African American communities.

Documents written by their former master Robert Collins reinforce on a personal level how slaves' marriages, like that of the Crafts, were manipulated by slaveholders for purposes of oppression and control, and how obtaining freedom did not buffer them from such interventions. In an essay on slave management, Collins did admit grudging admiration for what he had observed as "a *degree of* [emphasis mine] faithfulness, fidelity, and affection" among enslaved husbands and wives. He advised, "Taking wives and husbands among their fellow-servants [at] home should be as much encouraged as possible; and although intermarrying with those belonging to other estates should not be prohibited, yet it is always likely to lead to difficulties and troubles."[35] Once the Crafts were in England, as if to test the extent to which Collins truly valued the stabilizing and comforting qualities of marriage over the financial and social power obtained by owning other human beings, abolitionists submitted inquiries about purchasing the fugitives. Collins nixed the plan as far as his property was concerned, observing that "Ellen has been, from her youth, the most trusted and the most faithful of my house-servants; and in consequence, my family were very much attached to her. My object has been, not so much to enslave her again, as by recovering her to deter others from following her example . . . I prefer, as far as practicable, to exercise my own discretion in regard to bettering the condition of my slaves."[36]

In November 1850, Collins had requested publicly that President Millard Fillmore exert pressure on the city of Boston to uphold the Fugitive Slave Law and remand Ellen back to him. The president's secretary, W. S. Derrick, replied by providing reassurances that "wherever the laws of the United States shall be opposed, or the execution thereof obstructed in any state . . . it would be [the president's] duty to call forth the militia, and use the army and navy for the purpose of overcoming such forcible combinations against the laws." In such appeals to "legal officials," Collins clarified, he merely had intended to learn "whether a fugitive slave could be arrested in your city by the proper officers" and "whether after arrest . . . the judiciary would give judgment thereupon according to the law."[37] It is the law that Collins emphasizes in these offerings. His silence surrounding William and Ellen's marriage underscores his inability to comprehend such a thing outside of his dominion. Marriage among enslaved men and women is acceptable to Collins insofar as they remain enslaved, surveilled by a master like himself and vulnerable to his decisions come time to divide them.

The postings of William and Ellen Craft contrast with Collins's fixation on the government's execution of the Fugitive Slave Law and frustration at his inability to regulate the movements of his "property." Their updates to family and friends, addressed primarily from the south of England, where they began to obtain an education at the Ockham School, are characterized by the language of marriage and parenthood.[38] Characteristically, they mention their sons produced from their happy union on English soil. Their ability to escape slavery not only has challenged the southern patriarchy, it also has been a key to cementing an idea of marriage that challenges the legalistic and economic discourse that Collins aired.

The larger social networks beyond their marriage that the Crafts describe in *Running a Thousand Miles for Freedom* anticipate Harriet A. Jacobs's *Incidents in the Life of a Slave Girl*, which would be published a year later in the Boston they had fled. The historian Jean Fagan Yellin has remarked that Jacobs's autobiographical narrator Linda Brent "locates herself firmly within a social matrix" where "successive generations" of her black family members work to free each other, and where a wide circle of black and white activists both North and South participate in "an ongoing struggle for freedom" and an ongoing cycle of "concealment and escape."[39] William and Ellen partnered with reformers black and white, male and female, British and American, and these bonds grew deeper as these reformers crisscrossed the Atlantic carrying reports and correspondence of their progress.

With several free African American men such as the businessman Lewis Hayden and lawyer Robert Morris, white abolitionist men of Boston had formed the biracial Vigilance Committee, which specialized in throwing bounty hunters from the South off the scent of fugitives in the city. A black Philadelphian, Robert Purvis (1810–98), had aided the Crafts in adjusting to freedom by spiriting them to the household of a Quaker farming family: Barkley Ivens, his wife, and their children.[40] A white Bostonian and Vigilance Committee member, Francis Jackson (1789–1861), had presented the Crafts with money raised by the abolitionists for fares and expenses from Boston to Portland, Portland to Halifax, and Halifax to Liverpool. A raft of "respectable colored families" had stood at the ready to furnish rooms and meals to the couple when an innkeeper got cold feet about lodging them.[41] When the couple finally made it to England in 1851, they carried a letter signed by Unitarian minister Samuel May, a white Bostonian.[42] It was then a cohort of white British men and women who meticulously implemented a scheme for their education and who helped them decompress psychologically and physically from the suitcase life they had lived as fugitives on the run.

Interactions between the Crafts and British and American citizens in *Running a Thousand Miles for Freedom* acknowledge past collaborations that have reached across differences of ethnicity and race. They also foreshadow those that will extend well past this 1860 narrative. Given the transatlantic nature of their journey, it is not surprising that the Crafts are politic about commending both American and British friends for their assistance as they acclimated to the unfamiliar and at times unsettling demands of their years in the US North (December 1848–November 1850), as they then hurried through Canada in order "to leave the mock-free Republic," and then as they settled at Surrey's Ockham School where they would "acquire a little of that education which we were so shamefully deprived of while in bondage."[43] In part two of their memoir, which moves from the aftermath of their escape from Georgia through their departure and journey to Liverpool, such diplomatic articulations of gratitude, which heap praise on allies on both sides of the Atlantic, are numerous. As William, for example, remembers his and Ellen's hair's-breadth escape from agents of their old slave owners who had come to Boston to reclaim them, he exclaims, "Oh! May God bless the thousands of unflinching, disinterested abolitionists of America, who are laboring through evil as well as through good report, to cleanse their country's escutcheon from the foul and destructive blot of slavery, and to restore to every bondman his God-given rights; and may God ever smile upon England and upon England's good, much-beloved, and deservedly honored Queen, for the generous protection that is given to unfortunate refugees of every rank, and of every colour and clime."[44] This encomium depicts American and British allies as united with the slaves through their recognition of a higher, moral law that places goodness and the soul's salvation above humanity's arbitrary and shifting divisions of class, race, and national affiliation.

However, as John Ernest has very carefully argued in his interpretation of the memoir, *Running a Thousand Miles for Freedom* is "a narrative that indicts the contradictions and instabilities inherent in white-supremacist thought and culture far more than it does the system of slavery."[45] Foregoing the simple task of bifurcating America into racists and non-racists, and abolitionists and slaveholders, the Crafts deplore the entire national character. Even as they give examples of effective transatlantic partnerships in the antislavery battle, their memoir singles out America and Americans as the paragon of racial and ethnic nastiness.[46]

The Crafts also note the "[p]rejudice against colour" and other examples of "vulgar prejudice" among Atlantic Canadians they met and associate this squarely with the national psyche of the United States. For instance, in the provincial capital and port city of Halifax, Nova Scotia, when representatives of the Cunard Line "shamefully" give William the runaround as he attempts to purchase steamer tickets for England, he compares their rebuffs to the "mean Yankee excuses" that justify racial bias in the United States. Similarly, it is "the influence of low Yankee prejudice" that instigates the white female landlord of a "miserable, dirty hole" of an inn in Halifax to ask the couple to leave when she realizes that Ellen, who she has assumed is white, is the wife of "the dark man downstairs," William. The landlady uses the N-word, which the first part of the narrative has presented as the salient discursive marker of American proslavery communities, as does a "big, crotchety" coach driver whose "head" symbolically gets "stuck in the mud" as he attempts to unmoor the conveyance during a rainstorm. Finally, the memoir pointedly concludes with the statement that "the Americans, as a people, are notoriously mean and cruel towards all coloured persons, whether they are bond or free."[47]

If the "unflinching, disinterested abolitionists of America" merit equal praise as "England's good, much beloved, and deservedly honored Queen," elsewhere in its second half *Running a Thousand Miles for Freedom* carefully places responsibility on the entire United States for driving "the spirit of liberty and humanity out of . . . noble and generous-hearted men." Since they had lived in England for nine years before they brought out their popular book, and since they had secured a London publisher to do so, the Crafts must have been very aware of how much they had benefited from the hospitality, generosity, and kindness of British friends dedicated to the abolition of American slavery. The Civil War may have seemed imminent at this time to many transatlantic writers and readers, especially in light of the sectarian tensions that had escalated in the wake of John Brown's failed 1859 raid on the federal arsenal at Harper's Ferry, Virginia. Yet the Crafts, as well as other American fugitives in England and Europe, had no definite way of gauging whether such a mighty conflict would finally ignite, as much as they may have hoped one day to be forever "free from every slavish fear." Nevertheless, it seems inadequate and simplistic to blame their anti-American sentiments solely on a heightened sense of obligation and loyalty to the "extreme kindness" of their British hosts, especially in light of their eventual decision to return to the American South. By modeling the idea of transatlantic antislavery collaboration only to seemingly smash this model, the Crafts contribute to what Ernest defines as "self-organizing narrative representations of the complex and unstable racial order of the United States at mid century."[48]

Upon careful examination of the paratextual evidence in this section of *Running a Thousand Miles for Freedom*, one finds a similar combination of evenhanded testimony and praise for the American and British citizens who succor and provide asylum to the Crafts and, on the other hand, a rhetoric that links racial prejudice squarely with the American character. In a letter of introduction for the Crafts dated November 6, 1850, addressed to the ailing British abolitionist John Bishop Estlin (1785–1855), their friend Samuel May tells "my plain, sad story" of the hide-and-seek chase or hunt that ensued in Boston between William and Ellen and the "Messrs. Hughes and Knight, the slave-catchers," who had camped out in the city "'till they got hold of the niggers" and were able to fetch them back to Georgia. He credits the eventual departure of such "mercenary and unprincipled" men to "the vigilance of many persons who were on the look-out for them," and he muses that the US marshal never served the Crafts' arrest warrant, "perhaps through fear, for a general feeling of indignation, and a cool determination not to allow this young couple to be taken from Boston into slavery, was aroused, and pervaded the city." May finds an equally worthy champion of the couple's rights to freedom in his English correspondent across the water. "I am sure," he writes to Estlin, "if you were stretched on your bed in your last illness, and could lift your hand at all, you would extend it to welcome these poor hunted fellow creatures."[49]

Yet May upsets this evenhanded approach to the "kind words and deeds" of American and English activists by singling out the United States to receive the lion's share of blame for how African Americans have been victimized: "Oh! Shame, shame upon us, that Americans, whose fathers fought against Great Britain, in order to be FREE, should have to acknowledge this disgraceful fact! God gave us a fair and goodly heritage in this land, but man has cursed it with his devices and crimes against human souls and human rights. . . . A brave young man and a virtuous young woman must fly the American shores, and seek, under the shadow of the British throne, the enjoyment of 'life, liberty, and the pursuit of happiness.'" It is not merely against the measure of Great Britain that May finds America lacking. He even holds the "unprincipled and tyrannical Yankees" up to the world's mirror with disappointing results. As he writes to Estlin, "The laws of this republican and Christian land (tell it not in Moscow, nor in Constantinople) regard [the Crafts] only as slaves—chattels—personal property."[50]

Certainly the "burning shame" that May expresses in his letter for the land that "is not worthy of" the Crafts, and William and Ellen's own vilification of the racist American character that has produced such a country, reflects a conventional technique in antislavery literature.[51] I would also argue that, when placed in tandem with the praise for cross-racial collaborations that threads throughout *Running a Thousand Miles for Freedom*, this rhetoric constructs what Benedict Anderson identifies as an "imagined community" of black and white activists united not by national allegiances to a land and a flag but by compulsion to actualize universal principles of freedom and justice.[52]

Another paratextual reference earlier in the memoir anticipates this understanding of cross-racial, transnational communities of activists. William recollects how, on the night of their escape, he took Ellen "by the hand" and tentatively "peeped out" of the door of her cottage, such privacy being a privilege conferred upon her as a result of her exalted position in the hierarchy of house slaves as "a ladies' maid." He remembers, "I locked the door with my own key, which I now have before me, and tiptoed across the yard into the street."[53]

From a twenty-first-century perspective, it is extraordinary and moving to contemplate that some twelve years after fleeing from slavery, William sat under English protection, still in possession of and gazing at the actual, visceral key to their former domicile in American bondage, for nothing the Crafts had bought, received, or created for their little cottage belonged to them, not even their own bodies. His jarring disclosure invites comparison to the public exhibitions of other material objects and corporeal parts such as the black Henry Brown's box and panorama, and the white Jonathan Walker's branded hand.[54] According to HollyGale Millette, for black bodies, such "public displays of slavery in America" featured "scars, wounds and other signs of torture" that served both to re-inscribe and eroticize servitude and slavery back onto the fugitive's body.[55] Such emotionally wrenching visual symbols on the antislavery stage materialized the "human depravity" and trauma of the peculiar institution that activists such as the Crafts accused even the kindest of slaveholders and even the mildest forms of slavery of being complicit in sustaining.[56] They demonstrated the heroic lengths that both black and white persons would travel in order to claim themselves and externalize their resolve to resist victimization.

As William confesses, "I wish to present the system in its mildest form, and to show that the 'tender mercies of the wicked are cruel.'"[57] His key suggests the existential boundaries between slavery and freedom, objectification and humanity, immorality and respectability, and silence and assertion that he and Ellen have transgressed, as well as the physical border they crossed that divided the "thousand miles of slave territory" from the "flickering lights in the distance" which beckoned out of Philadelphia, their "first city of refuge" in the free states, and dazzled their "dim eyes."[58] It is 1860 when *Running a Thousand Miles for Freedom* appears at a bookstall on London's 337 Strand, and the Crafts' cottage key is useless, not merely because they have made a new home in England. They now belong to a community of activists as intimate as "our relatives," and their citizenship in this community derives not from place or inheritance, from where they were born, or whether their parents were enslaved or free, but from their shared commitment to dismantling slavery.[59]

Williams Wells Brown groomed the Crafts on the expectations and etiquette of public antislavery meetings as he had done in America. The *Bristol Mercury* of August 30, 1851, reported that Brown and both of the Crafts had "attended a considerable number of public meetings in Scotland, in the north of England, and in some of the midland counties, and those of the south-west of the island (where they had the opportunity of diffusing a large amount of information upon American slavery, and of acquiring many friends)."[60] On February 12, 1851, the *Aberdeen Journal* advertised a lecture by Brown "(assisted by WILLIAM CRAFT—whose wife, ELLEN CRAFT, the 'White Slave,' will also be present—)." The two men also promised spectators that their talk would be "enlivened by the Recital of ANTI-SLAVERY MELODIES," very likely showing off one of Brown's original antislavery compositions.[61] Brown reflected to Craft the respected activist he aspired to become, and Craft matched Brown as a living repository of enslavement's unforgettable miseries.

From the early 1850s through the mid-1860s, the Crafts worked together with the British antislavery community to represent themselves as symbols of self-help and inner resourcefulness. First, as the slavery question increased political tensions in the United States, and then as the Civil War disrupted transatlantic markets, these American and British abolitionist friends used newspapers to present the Crafts before reading publics on both sides of the ocean as hardworking, self-starting, clever, and independent. As the *Leeds Mercury* reported, the Crafts "came not, however, to us as destitute suppliants for our alms; they were able and willing to work for their support; though they thankfully accepted the boon of education." "The Crafts," echoed Bristol's *Mercury*, "have no means but their own exertions to look to for future support."[62]

Nineteenth-century British audiences admired William's insistence on pulling his own weight even if his allies had his back. Thus, in her 1865 reader *The Freedmen's Book*, Lydia Maria Child, the self-described "old friend" of the emancipated slaves, dedicated a long biographical essay to the Crafts. She mentions William's expeditions to Africa from 1862 to 1869.[63] A coalition of British Quakers, abolitionists, and businessmen had outfitted him to sail to what is now Benin, to persuade kings "in that stronghold of the African slave trade" to deter the violence and warfare generated by the trafficking of human bodies in favor of the more peaceful production of cotton, which they could sell to European textile markets in exchange for manufactured items.[64] Because of the disruptions of the Civil War, the pace of agricultural production in the American South had dissipated. Craft's commercial venture would engender new Atlantic routes, and the cotton would keep spinning on the looms of England's mill and factory towns, even as Union troops ravaged the croplands of the American South.

According to Child, it was William Craft's "honesty, energy, and good sense" that had inspired "so much respect and confidence in England" that he had been entrusted on this "very important" mission with "a valuable cargo of goods." "He is now," she concluded, "one of the most enterprising and respected merchants in that part of the world. . . . How much would have been lost to himself and the world if he had remained a slave in Georgia, not allowed to profit by his own industry, and forbidden to improve his mind by learning to read!" Child holds up William to his fellow African Americans as a model of initiative and literacy, who, now that Jubilee has dawned, vindicates the necessity of both.[65]

However, as much as sympathetic transatlantic writers represented William Craft as plucky, ambitious, and industrious, they also seemed to impose upon him meanings that risked undermining his goal of "elevating people of his own color."[66] Transcribing one of his speeches in the third-person, stenographic fashion of the time, the *Bristol Mercury* reported that

> [Mr. Craft] said he felt himself that evening placed in a very serious position indeed, when he looked back and saw that it was only two years since his wife and himself were slaves in the state of Georgia . . . and then when he looked at their position at the present time, and found they were as free as the freest, and that they were in the midst of friends. . . . But when he reflected upon what his relations, and his

friends and fellow-men were still suffering in the United States, he could not help saying a few words on their behalf, even though these words should be ungrammatical (cheers).[67]

The *Bristol Mercury*'s report ostensibly places the liberated William in the position of being empowered to advocate with his voice for the millions of still-enslaved Africans. By encouraging readers to visualize the "suffering" of his "friends and fellow-men" in a distant time and place, it emphasizes the new status that he and Ellen have attained by slipping the yoke of slavery. Yet it also singles out William's "ungrammatical" speech, as if to suggest that his newfound agency is effective not because he is now "as free as the freest" but because, as one who still bears the markers of oppression, he can stand as proxy for other Africans still in bondage, to inspire pity, outrage, and gestures of charity among those who have come to see and hear him.[68]

Writing back to transatlantic readers from his West African expeditions, William asserts a somewhat different model for building coalitions with black "friends and fellow-men," one that tempers conventional notions of Africans' oppression and their need for deliverance, held by his allies in the reform movement, with attitudes that deviate from that script. One representative example of his deviant standpoint appears in a public report of his "partial success" persuading the leaders of various cities and towns to cultivate cotton rather than trade slaves and make war over slaves. In this public letter, published in the *Caledonian Mercury* of July 3, 1863, William seems to have internalized the assumptions of the British friends he has met during his travels, such as "Mr. Mann, clergyman of the English Church society," that Africans are not a saved people, and that, business intentions aside, he should take advantage of every opportunity to bring them from the darkness of paganism to the light of Christianity. At one missionary outpost, he is delighted to have dinner with "a native clergyman," who he describes as "a very excellent man" and "devoted to his work," yet he shares his disappointment with the *Mercury*'s readers at finding that his companion has converted "few communicants." Similarly, at an English fort "in the notorious" slave-trading center of Whydah, he encounters the "Rev. Mr. Benasko," who "has a chapel in the yard, but I am sorry to say it is not numerously attended."[69]

William inflects this judgment about the spiritual indifference of Whydah's denizens with baffled descriptions of the polygamous relationships that he observed. In the compound of one king, he saw "an elevated place adjoining the walls for the King's two or three hundred wives to promenade; but, strange to say . . . sometimes these 'better halves' are in silks and velvets, sitting around the King, then again dressed in cotton-cloth and trading in the market-place." Without considering these relationships in the context of values and a worldview that may differ from those of the Western Hemisphere but are just as viable and sustaining, William embraces the conventional opinion that Africans are religious prodigals in urgent need of a rescuer, preferably English, who can lead them to Christian enlightenment. He frames his journey as cultural as well as commercial work, just like his white British colleague and fellow member of the London Emancipation Society, Frederick William Chesson (1833–88), who cofounded the group. Chesson introduces William's letter and supports his reliance on "moral instrumentalities" during this mission "to ameliorate the condition of his African brethren." He endorses William's venture by stating that "[f]ounded, as the hideous 'customs' of West Africa are, upon the grossest popular superstitions (and not, as is often supposed, upon the sanguinary cruelty of a few despotic chiefs), they can only be overthrown by the combined influence of commerce and Christianity."[70]

William also attempts to define his relationship to the Africans on his own terms, outside of the social and cultural stereotypes that even abolitionists were not immune to. "May God be pleased," he exclaims, "soon to christianize this heathen, though not altogether savage, people!" His differentiation of "heathen" or "unsaved," from "savage" or "bestial," rhymes with Chesson's distinction between Africans' "superstitions," which can be debunked and replaced with Christian belief, and perceptions that they are innately predatory, bloodthirsty, and quick to kill, which apply only to a few. Yet, while both men direct a theme of correction to the "the negro character on the West Coast of Africa," William turns this admonishment back upon the

English, and he uses the voices of the Africans themselves to do it. In a meeting with "the King of Porto Novo," William writes,

> Among other things, he said that the English have treated him with great cruelty and injustice in burning his town and killing a great number of his people without provocation; and for fear of a repetition of this cruelty, he said that he had placed his country in the hands of the French for protection. His Majesty also stated, that among all the English he had but one friend, and that was Captain Davies. Captain Davies kindly gave me a letter of introduction to the King, which was read by his Majesty's interpreter, a native trader, who speaks, reads, and writes English well. After a long conversation respecting the advantages of legitimate trade and the cultivation of cotton in particular, the King finally said that his people were now engaged in the production of palm-oil, and did not understand the cultivation of cotton; and as he had given his country to the French, he had no power, at present, to carry out my suggestions.

The king's "native" trader who is fluent in English suggests a confident agenda by and for Africans that the earlier image of an "ungrammatical" William, apologetic to the audience for his deficiencies on the antislavery stage, cannot.[71]

The Africans have their own priorities—here, finding a European ally who will not massacre them like the English and nourishing their palm-oil trade—that take precedence over the antislavery campaign of William and those back home in the British Isles who funded him. They are respectful of the agenda that William places before them on behalf of his work with English antislavery friends, but they do not care to ponder it. William's recognition of the Africans' self-determination in this correspondence anticipates his own entrepreneurial and educational scheme, funded by antislavery friends but conceived and executed by himself, that would begin seven years later. Where his partnerships with English friends to transform Dahomey met with mixed results he would later revive old antislavery alliances only to see his scheme, and many of these alliances, dragged under.

CHAPTER FOUR

The Boston Libel Trial of William Craft

> The educational problem, which the liberation and
> enfranchisement of the negroes created, was in all respects
> peculiar and in some respects very difficult of solution. When
> the negroes became citizens, especially in those states in
> which they constituted nearly or quite half the population, the
> obvious thing to do, in the interest of everybody concerned,
> was to educate them, that they might become good rather
> than bad citizens, intelligent voters and worthy members
> of society rather than an ignorant and possibly dangerous
> part of the population. But it was not so easy to say how this
> could be accomplished.
> —"*Two Schools for Negroes*" (*1876*)

By 1870, William and Ellen Craft had returned to the United States
with their children, having realized the loving family they had dreamed
of (see figures 6, 7, and 8 for images of three of their five children). In
their next two decades in America, they would answer public and personal calls to uplift the collective bodies and minds of black southerners. This idea of collective duty is implicit in the themes of love and
liberty that merge in the couple's speaking, writing, and activism. In
the mid-1870s, however, a very public entanglement of suspicions and
accusations reminded them, who needed no such reminding, that in a
postbellum South where the terms between African Americans and
white Americans had shifted, their focus on the intellectual and economic liberation of their people invited obstruction and sabotage. The
archival record of the conflict that impugned William Craft's name
and reputation points to how he and Ellen serve as metonyms for the

Figure 6. Charles Craft, son, from William and Ellen Craft's photograph album (ca. 1850s). Craft and Crum families collection. Photo courtesy of the Avery Research Center for African American History and Culture, College of Charleston, Charleston, S.C.

meandering routes African American communities traveled toward full citizenship and freedom.

With pledges in hand from luminaries such as Harriet Martineau (1802–76), whose writings had alerted British readers to the injustices of American slavery, William planned to knock on the doors of old New England allies in order to raise monies to establish "a first-class free school for the colored children belonging to the people."[1] His qualifications for this task came of his previous experience as an educator, having tutored other students at Ockham in the 1850s and founded a school for youth in Whydah in the 1860s.[2] He would seek moral and material support from Americans who had championed him and Ellen back in 1850, sequestered them from slave catchers,

Figure 7. Ellen Craft, daughter, from William and Ellen Craft's photograph album (ca. 1850s). Craft and Crum families collection. Photo courtesy of the Avery Research Center for African American History and Culture, College of Charleston, Charleston, S.C.

and secured their safe passages to Canada and England, as well as from British allies who had opened homes and hearts to the fugitive couple and helped educate them and prepare them to work and live independently.

In 1870, during joyful reunions with members of the old antislavery communities from Boston, Cambridge, and other Boston suburbs, William raised "a small fund," augmented by money from "a few good friends in England," to begin erection of a cooperative farm and school.[3] The bloodiest war that the country had ever known, the wrenching cases of fugitive slaves such as Anthony Burns (1834–62), and the martyrdoms of John Brown (1800–59) and Colonel Robert Gould Shaw (1837–63) had New England reformers eager to revive

Figure 8. Alfred Craft, son, from William and Ellen Craft's photograph album (ca. 1850s). Craft and Crum families collection. Photo courtesy of the Avery Research Center for African American History and Culture, College of Charleston, Charleston, S.C.

their old activism. British reformers too jumped at an opportunity to take out subscriptions for such a worthy-sounding plan as setting freed people on paths to literacy, employment, and self-reliance.

After talking to William, one British booster for the project enthused in the *Glasgow Herald*, "To produce cotton and sugar . . . in the quantities which these rich lands are capable of producing them, demands (as under the slave system) culture on a large scale, and implements too expensive for freedmen to buy. Cooperation has, therefore, become necessary."[4] The word "cooperation" carries two meanings here, indicating William's vision of freed people pooling their land and labor to build wealth and also implying how their connections with transatlantic activists could make this wealth-building happen.

In spite of support, the Crafts initially floundered. By 1871, the Ku Klux Klan had burned to a shambles Hickory Hill, the first farm and school they established near Savannah, Georgia.[5] Two years later, in the summer of 1873, a resilient William briskly solicited seven thousand dollars from Bostonians to purchase eighteen hundred acres of farmland they were leasing for a new, "self-supporting" agricultural school "at Woodville, in Bryan County, nineteen miles from Savannah, on the Atlanta and Gulf Railroad."[6]

With the promise of a teacher from the American Missionary Association, the Crafts hoped that Woodville Cooperative Farm School would provide its initial "seventeen children, belonging to the six families who worked on the place" with "a chance of getting at least the rudiments of education" in a state where schools for African Americans were "mostly if not entirely confined to towns." William wrote to prospective donors, "We propose that the children should attend school part of the time, and work on the land the remainder. By this means they can grow vegetables and grain enough for their own use. The parents of the children on the place will have to rent land, as elsewhere, and pay a portion of their crop, which will go to assist the school."[7]

Between 1874 and 1876, as he made the rounds of potential benefactors, William called upon Rufus Ellis, the secretary of the Society for the Propagation of the Gospel, a religious organization founded in the colonial era that helped finance such southern industrial schools as Hampton Institute (Virginia), Tuskegee (Alabama), and Claflin (South Carolina). These institutions trained Native Americans and African Americans primarily in skilled manual labor and domestic arts so as to partner in reviving the South's wrecked post–Civil War economy, while assuring white southerners that their pupils posed no threat to their domination of business and politics. William called upon former antislavery activists for assistance too, such as lawyers George Stillman Hillard (1808–79) and Samuel Edmund Sewall (1799–1888), William Lloyd Garrison, Lydia Maria Child, the statesman Charles Sumner (1811–74), Rev. James Freeman Clarke, and Rev. Edward Everett Hale (1822–1909), whose statue now greets visitors at the gates of Boston's public gardens. During an 1875 visit to Hale's church, the number of tenants at Woodville had doubled to "fifteen or sixteen families." "About seventy pupils" attended classes taught by both Ellens, mother and daughter, in a frame schoolhouse, "a story and a half high, well lighted by windows." "Religious services were held in the schoolhouse, either by the Methodists or Baptists," and the senior Ellen gave Sunday school lessons there. On the grounds that "his plan was not a charitable but rather a self-sustaining one," William declined the offers of "articles of clothing and food tendered by the ladies" of Hale's church.[8]

Tensions and vitriol increased in Georgia in the wake of William's frequent trips up north to Massachusetts. In April 1878, he was back in his old Boston stomping grounds, not to manage money coming in but instead to mount a libel suit in Suffolk County's Supreme Court. He was plaintiff against Sebastian Barthold Schlesinger (1837–1917) and other defendants in Naylor and Company, a manufacturing firm dealing in iron and steel, who backed their statements against William with "the affidavits of a number of Georgians and the testimony of some Bostonians."[9]

William's tract of land, in what once was known as the "Breadbasket of the Confederacy," straddled the coastal empire of the Arnold family, whose patriarch, Richard James Arnold of Rhode Island (1796–1873), had owned some of the most prosperous rice plantations in tidewater Georgia. Arnold and other Bryan County planters had temporarily been dispossessed of their lands due to General Sherman's Special Field Order Number 15. Yet by 1867 their ownership had been largely restored. One of the Crafts' white neighbors, George Appleton, had married Arnold's granddaughter Luly. Perhaps an assumption of entitlement to Woodville, and an attitude of outrage about "uppity" freedpeople had inspired Appleton to persuade one of Woodville's benefactors, Schlesinger, to denounce William in the northern papers as "sailing under false colors." Schlesinger, who also was a classical composer and German consul to Boston, had been one of the city's residents who had responded with "open arms and cordial sympathy" to William's appeals for charitable assistance. Now Schlesinger accused William and his family of "liv[ing] on the money he collects every summer," saying that "*not one cent* of it goes to any charitable purpose."[10]

With Woodville on the line, William sued for slander. In September 1876, William's complaint alleged, Schlesinger had published letters "in the *Boston Daily Advertiser* and other Boston papers [such as the *Herald*, *Globe*, *Traveller*, and *Post*]," as well as the New York *Sun* and Savannah *Morning News*, that had accused "the colored man, William Craft" of misappropriating funds. Three men, two of them white—the sheriff of Bryan County (Charles A. Batchellor) and the county school commissioner (J. B. Smith)—and an African American man named James Andrews (acting as a justice of the peace) had signed the notices. They accused William Craft of being an "impostor" and "humbug" and of spending "not one cent" of the money he had raised for the purposes he had stated. As a result of these communiqués, some of William's "warmest supporters afterwards treated him in a very cool manner, and he and his school both were suffering in consequence." For the injuries sustained to his character and reputation, William demanded ten thousand dollars in damages. The court conducted a hearing for eight days, from June 6–14, and handed down its judgment on June 16, 1878. Dismissing his complaint, three referees or ombudsmen added insult to injury by ordering William to pay a portion of the defendants' legal fees.[11]

The testimony against William Craft suggests that resentment about a black man with money and influence, exacerbated by his own limited knowledge about farming, may have fed at least one northern supporter's latent skepticism about him. This wariness recalls pre–Civil War anxieties about free African Americans who fraudulently passed themselves off as fugitive slaves to unsuspecting abolitionists in order to receive alms or donations. In the twelfth and final chapter of her 1859 novel *Our Nig*, the African American author Harriet E. Wilson (1825–1900) fictionalized such a charlatan, whose back "showed no marks of the lash." His "illiterate harangues were humbugs for hungry abolitionists."[12] Similarly, the white Bryan County school commissioner J. B. Smith remarked that "he did not see how [William] could carry on an industrial school in Georgia and live in Boston as much as [he] did." Leverett Saltonstall, a colleague of William's friend George S. Hillard, recalled how William left his office "with a sneer on his face, as he said to me, 'Give me money! A few hundreds to be sure, a few hundreds! You call that a large amount, do you?' as if [according to Saltonstall] he was in the habit of handling them by the thousands of millions."[13]

Smith's and Saltonstall's comments indicate how the Crafts may have successfully reinvented themselves as social elites during their exile in the British Isles. The "darlings of the fugitive slave narrative circuit in Britain," writes the cultural historian HollyGale Millette, the Crafts "seemed to be courting the favor of moneyed yet conscientious classes." Their well-to-do associates, she writes, had helped them find a "comfortable middle-class Victorian home" in well-heeled West London and enroll as pupils in the Ockham School "when education and academic pursuits . . . were still strongly the preserve of the upper and middle classes."[14] This opportunistic acculturation to the British middle and upper classes may have endowed the Crafts with attitudes and expectations that irritated or surprised their fellow American citizens, including other abolitionists.

Another factor that may have contributed to William's alienation from many former alliances may have been "a rhetoric of martial manhood" that the Civil War historian Carole Emberton has observed. Politicians and policy makers who appropriated this rhetoric predicated freedom and citizenship on military service. Soldiering and a soldier's values of hard work, discipline, honesty, and devotion to family members and other dependents were seen as "a direct path to manhood" for most American men. To secure the ballot and to subscribe to respectable gender roles, African American men and women would insert this rhetoric in their discourse of racial uplift.[15] William Craft had not fought in the Civil War, in comparison to prominent African American men such as Frederick Douglass's son Charles Remond (1844–1920) and the novelist Martin Robison Delaney (1812–85), who earned distinction as the first black field officer in the Union Army. Although he had been residing in England or teaching and trading on the African continent during the Civil War, his lack of military service when so many had fallen for the Union called his integrity and character, and those of his wife Ellen and adult sons, into question.

During William's trial, Ellen Craft was called to the stand by William's lawyers for friendly cross-examination. The story she tells of Woodville School, repeated in the customary third-person perspective of nineteenth-century reportage, is a triumphal narrative that asserts her role as a respectable wife and respected teacher. She describes Woodville in the early 1870s as a plantation "in wretched condition, the houses miserable holes, dirty and full of rats and snakes, the plantation unfenced and all run over with weeds." By 1875, Woodville's tenants had grown to "fifteen or sixteen families," including "thirty" school-aged children, who gradually had restored order to the buildings and grounds. By 1878, according to Ellen, "the whole appearance of things had been changed. The new buildings had been built, and all the old ones repaired." Ellen, or "Mrs. Craft" as the papers called her, invited social approval and talked back to those who may have implicated her as the pampered beneficiary of William's alleged fraud. Her narrative cast her in the gendered role of a "ministering angel among the afflicted," bringing medicines to the sick, distributing food and clothing to the indigent, teaching the women to sew and to be "tidy and neat . . . so that they might become good wives and mothers." "There had been no arrests for stealing and fighting," she testifies. She even "had succeeded in breaking up the habit of whipping the children by substituting the plan that when the parents wanted to whip them, they should take them out in the graveyard, and there they would often kneel down and pray." "The moral character of all the people had been greatly improved," Ellen confesses, and she presents herself as both the modest servant who has effected that improvement and the moral guardian nearby, ensuring that it sticks.[16]

Ellen's testimony points to the limitations of the politics of respectability as a blunting force against racial bigotry. Ellen describes bringing "between two or three thousand dollars" back from England for the education of freedpeople, including a six-hundred-dollar gift from Lady Byron, whose daughter, Augusta Ada King, Countess of Lovelace (1815–52), had founded Ockham School, where Ellen and William had learned to read and write. Exemplifying what the sympathetic *Boston Daily Advertiser* describes as "[o]ne peculiar characteristic of the colored race" and "the instinct of a hunted being that had been developed and inherited in slavery," Ellen "persistently" declines, according to the paper, to say what she has done with the money. She confides that "she regarded the gift as so sacred that she did not even tell her husband what she did with it." What may be understood as an African American woman's prerogative to protect aspects of her personal life risked misinterpretation in the press as the same kind of mendacity and disingenuousness that had landed William on the wrong side of former friends and advocates. The *Daily Advertiser* had been sympathetic to the antislavery cause and had printed articles on behalf of the humanity and right to freedom of the enslaved. By reducing Ellen Craft in print to a bundle of "inherited" instincts rather than intellect, however, the paper again demonstrates how progressive white northerners who crusaded for the welfare of women and African Americans could not necessarily extricate themselves from their culture's more condescending perceptions about gender and race.[17]

Ellen's wit, however, does complicate this exchange and leaves her with a sort of even hand, if not the upper one. Her son Brougham, the court is told, happens to be Lady Byron's godson. Reading between the lines, Ellen seems aware of how this bond between an English peer and two fugitives from slavery, in exile from the United States for almost twenty years, may suggest to the court that she and William are outliers in relation to the society and culture of Reconstruction Era America. So she confides that she does not "trust" her money "to savings banks" but instead prefers to conceal her hard-earned coins and currency under the mattress or buried in the yard.[18] By assuming the confessional manner of someone close enough to the memories and privations of enslavement and war to be suspicious of the safety of banks and skeptical of the wealth that interest rates can build for an ordinary woman like her, Ellen performs the role of an innocent who would surely never collude with her husband to swindle people, white or black. She suggests that William likewise is an innocent, no crafty capitalist that his detractors have made him out to be. Her minstrel mask eases the tension, the room erupts in laughter, and she never does tell her examiner where the money went.

In spite of the levity that Ellen brought to the proceedings, the Crafts' former sponsors nevertheless helped derail William and Ellen's southern scheme and muddy William's character. Almost everyone who was anyone in the annals of abolition had been summoned as witnesses: Child, Garrison, Clarke, Hale, Underground Railroad conductor William Ingersoll Bowditch, and John Greenleaf Whittier, among others.[19] Some former admirers of William's independence and moral rectitude now took the stand to air their apprehensions. For example, Wendell Phillips, who had agitated against the effects of the 1850 Fugitive Slave Law on families like the Crafts, testified "that he had, at various times, given Craft money for the education and training of the colored people, although he had never approved his plan. After 1875, he refused to give Mr. Craft any more money, because he had found one of Craft's sons [Brougham], whom he had supposed to be assisting his father in Georgia, loafing about Washington and living on the money the father collected."[20]

In contrast to Phillips's damning testimony, other former donors remained loyal to William and Ellen and stolidly in William's corner. Samuel Sewall had been the executor of the funds William had raised, which he used to pay down Woodville's mortgage. By reminding the court that the school did not charge fees to students, and that the Crafts' oldest son, Charles, had received "small compensation for his services as one of Woodville's teachers," Sewall justified William's prodigious fund-raising in earlier years as crucial for Woodville's maintenance rather than a camouflage for spending sprees. "I believed his statements then," concluded Sewall, "and I believe them now."[21]

Perhaps it would come as no surprise if black Bostonians, like numbers of the Crafts' white donors, had distanced themselves from this case. If cultural and social differences owing to their years in England may have alienated the Crafts from former white allies in the United States, it stands that, with the mutual goal of rescuing William and Ellen from slave catchers no longer binding them and with the couple's good name in jeopardy, old friends from Boston's African American community may have deserted them now. In my examination of the case file in the Massachusetts Supreme Judicial Court Archives, I found only the names of prominent white male Bostonians subpoenaed to testify or to surrender potentially impugning documents. However, a receipt from the African American lawyer Robert Morris, an old friend of the Crafts, quietly narrates a story of loyalty and trust. Apparently, Morris put up funds to assist William in managing the costs of litigation, which the court duly noted. African American tenants from Woodville, the *Boston Daily Advertiser* reports, also traveled to the trial and testified on the stand to the prodigious effort the Crafts had undertaken and to their exhaustive application of money, prayers, and labor to their collective dream of domesticating an unruly backcountry property into an orderly farm and school.[22]

In the 1870s, William and Ellen's educational projects proved rocky, yet the usefulness of their saga for the edification of others would remain robust. The black Pennsylvanian and abolitionist William Still, for example, selected their story for his 1872 book *The Underground Rail Road*. His intention was that "[t]hose who come after us seeking for information in regard to the existence, atrocity, struggles and destruction of Slavery, will have no trouble in finding this hydra-headed monster . . . for at least several generations. Nor will posterity have any difficulty in finding the deeds of the brave and invincible opposers of Slavery."[23]

As if to demonstrate how the trajectory of African Americans since slavery rested on the abolitionists' model of collective effort and individual sacrifice, Still emphasized the role of the Underground Railroad in the Crafts' early flight from Georgia in 1848—a major deviation from their own account. As if to remind readers of the political limbo that Reconstruction Era African Americans still occupied, notwithstanding their attainments, Still devoted two-thirds of his story to the Crafts' brush with the Fugitive Slave Law. By retelling the Crafts' story, it was as if Still and his antislavery colleagues could push back their anxieties that younger American audiences at the century's end, including the nascent classes of what Du Bois would label the "new-issue Negro," would soon forgot the work of abolition.[24]

While the Crafts' agenda to educate the freedpeople reaped dwindling and disappointing results, their "thrilling" story of love, liberation, and escaping slavery continued to gain traction. Two years after the public undressing of his character, as William struggled to keep Woodville afloat, a group of white northern businessmen, ministers, lawyers, doctors, and other professionals, and of white women "of the highest character," signed and published a testimonial in which they affirmed their "undiminished confidence" in William and renewed their arrangements to finance his southern experiment.[25] As the Crafts' former compatriot Lydia Maria Child once wrote, "few white people have shown as much intelligence, moral worth, and refinement of feeling as the fugitive slaves William and Ellen Craft."[26] The outcome of William Craft's trial is a reminder that such fugitive lives were not always triumphant, in spite of the best efforts by the African Americans and their friends to remember them that way.

A Story to Pass Down

> Directly and indirectly, the fugitive slaves probably did more to
> bring about the abolition of slavery than any other one agency.
> The Northern people learned from the lips of these fugitives—
> from the strange, romantic, pathetic and tragic stories they
> told—that the slaves, no matter how ignorant or how different
> in colour or condition they might seem, were very much the
> same kind of human beings as themselves. They learned from
> the sufferings of these fugitives, from the desperate efforts
> which they made to escape, that no matter what might be said
> to the contrary the slaves wanted to be free.
> —*Booker T. Washington*, The Story of the Negro *(1909)*

Within a few years following the Boston suit, the troubled Woodville School fell into bankruptcy. Yet to end William and Ellen Craft's story with this disappointment and failure would be to ignore the legacy of community service, social improvement, and educational and political engagement that the Crafts bequeathed to their descendants. In 1883, for example, the Crafts' only daughter, Ellen, also married a man named William: the Charleston native William Demosthenes Crum (1859–1912), who, like her mother, was the biracial progeny of a southern white slaveholder. Crum, who earned a medical degree from Howard University, became a Reconstruction Era leader in the Republican Party and, in a throwback to William Craft's days on the West African coast, later was appointed minister to Liberia.[1]

The same year that this second-generation Ellen and William tied the knot, the Crafts' son Charles presented his parents with a grandchild, Henry Kempton Craft (1883–1974). He earned an undergraduate science degree from Harvard, taught classes in electrical science at Tuskegee University, and later served as a national administrator for the YMCA. He also followed in the socially committed example of his famous grandparents by serving in the Education Division of the New York State Commission against Discrimination.[2] Ironically, Henry did not learn their story until his teens, because his mother, Emeline Aubin Kinloch Craft (1854–1944), "had wanted to forget that whole episode. . . . She was not a slave, she had not gone through this and thought it was not something to be proud of."[3]

Henry Craft's wife, Elizabeth Letitia "Bessie" Trotter (1883–1949), was the sister of the famous African American journalist and civil rights crusader William Monroe Trotter (1872–1934). This connection intertwines the Crafts' family tree with that of Sally Hemings and President Thomas Jefferson, since Bessie descended from Sally's enslaved sister Mary. Another Harvard graduate, Trotter was the first African American elected to the honor society Phi Beta Kappa. With its themes of equality, education, and citizenship, his weekly political newspaper *The Guardian* (1901–50) was a toast to the activist spirit of the Crafts. In addition to its subject matter, Trotter's paper literally followed in the footsteps of William and Ellen and their antislavery friends, since its offices were housed where both the *Liberator* and *Uncle Tom's Cabin* had been published."[4]

Across the long transom of subsequent generations and more wars and social upheavals, what have the Crafts possibly left to the rest of us? In their escapes from slavery and from the nominally free North, their self-presentations in transatlantic antislavery publications, their reflections in their 1860 memoir about the ideologies and ironies of bondage and freedom, and their post–Civil War efforts to sustain the freedpeople by educating them and working to help them build their wealth and security, the Crafts can tell us something about how and why we still remember slavery. Their story certainly reiterates prominent themes that also resonate in other American fugitives' oral recollections, private correspondence, photographs, and published memoirs, such as the self-mastery and single-mindedness of Frederick Douglass; the relentless, savvy self-fashioning of Sojourner Truth (1797–1883); the collaborative spirit of Elizabeth Hobbs Keckley (1818–1907), who founded her own relief organization for the freedpeople; and the creative drive and cosmopolitan outlook of William Wells Brown, the Crafts' longtime friend and mentor.[5]

In addition, like those of so many other enslaved Africans, the Crafts' memory may have persisted in the popular imagination—onstage, for example, in Sherry Boone's off-Broadway production of *Ellen Craft: A New American Opera* (2004), and in the performances of individual historical re-enactors—because their story is quintessentially an American one. What their saga that begins in slavery says is that to be American is to believe in the second chance: the opportunity to pull oneself and one's loved ones from the wreckage of missed prospects, spectacular failures, or reckless gambles, and to resiliently begin again—wiser, stronger, sometimes a bit more cautiously, sometimes even more daring, outrageous, and path-breaking than before. Trying to revive his flagging literary career by taking a stab at the movie business, F. Scott Fitzgerald would express his angst about a culture that emphasized success and accomplishment and devalued the process of refining one's talents. "There are no second acts in American lives," he lamented.[6] The Crafts acted is if they believed otherwise. Even if they did not always fulfill their dreams, the Crafts kept trying.

When one escape did not provide the safety and security they craved, William and Ellen Craft ventured another. When one school was burned down, they erected a second. When lectures and public appearances did not fully support them financially, they turned to other projects, such as writing a memoir and brokering trade agreements with West African kingdoms. The Crafts increased the reach of their activism by partnering with British and American allies within antislavery, mechanics', and freedpeople's organizations. However, when an initiative seemed closed to them within these institutional structures, such as when veterans of antislavery organizations pulled away from supporting the Woodville School and their funds dried up, they demonstrated the qualities of the entrepreneur by going it alone rather than abandoning the opportunity. They took a page from their protean compatriot William Wells Brown, who excelled at the role that Rafia Zafar defines as "the trickster, the apparently powerless individual who manages to come out on top regardless of the opponent's strength."[7] To those of us in the twenty-first century who have listened to and taken delight in rappers like Jay-Z, Eminem, Fifty Cent, and others, often returning from defeat in their rhymes to vanquish internal demons and external adversaries, and to those of us who have rooted for celebrities like Jennifer Hudson as they move from grief or rejection to fortune, fame, and movie deals, the Crafts' examples of reinvention, of being down for the count but not out, of jumping back into the game when the game apparently seems over, are reassuring, seductive, and empowering.

Although William and Ellen did not literally experience the Middle Passage, the chapter of their lives that stands in some ways as its symbolic equivalent is their nearly twenty-year detour across the Atlantic in England. Compared to the fetid, festering decks, the miserable "little" piles "of dead people," and the "thrashing," "trembling," and "crouching" human cargo that the author Toni Morrison evokes as African Americans' collective memory of the Middle Passage, William and Ellen's long residency in England was a paradise.[8] They were not among the over ten million Africans kidnapped from their families and communities, marched in coffles to the coast, branded and tortured and assaulted and sorted in slave castles, and jammed in chains aboard slave ships for a transatlantic voyage.[9] Instead, they lived as a middle-class family with a bustling home and healthy children. They met and mingled with aristocrats, international activists, and celebrated artists. Yet, like their own enslaved ancestors in America, they did endure an unanticipated, rather abrupt journey across the Atlantic via ship, and during the nearly two decades they spent living in England they must have experienced the exile's anxiety about the future, grief about the past, and dislocation and unmooring from all that was customary.

As Americans, we are bound to and haunted by this collective legacy of enslavement and heartbreak, the dismemberment of families and communities during removals from Africa, the centuries of separations and divisions that the traffic in human bodies engendered in the Americas. Scholars such as Michael A. Gomez and Robert Farris Thompson have accomplished amazing, elegant work tracing cultural, linguistic, philosophical, and artistic retentions that survived the horrific ordeal.[10] Yet we still struggle to come to terms with this past and to liberate ourselves and our communities from its unwelcome descendants—racial bigotry, social intolerance, fear of and resistance to change—that have attached to us and will not let go. To exorcise them, we dedicate monuments and museums. Privileged descendants of slave traders, like the DeWolf family of Bristol, Rhode Island, wrestle with how best to make amends for this history, and elite universities such as Brown and Harvard, as well as southern schools such as Clemson University and the University of Virginia, deliberate about how best to reconcile their august reputations with the blunt truth that many of their founders were complicit in the lucrative, brutal slave trade.[11]

Our memory of the Crafts links with a desire to recover the lost voices of those who were enslaved and those who bought, sold, and owned them. It invites us to think about the polyvocal nature of African American literary history and how, as Eric Gardner writes, African American subjects like the Crafts actively and collaboratively shaped "black stories" written about them.[12] Like other genres of African American literature, such as the early periodicals that John Ernest examines, the exodus narratives that Rhondda Robinson Thomas traces, and the postbellum, book-length "race histories" that Laurie F. Maffly-Kipp has studied, the Crafts in their memoir *Running a Thousand Miles for Freedom* intended to write themselves and their fellow black Americans into a more complete "history, and thus a moral identity, for a people often characterized as lacking in both."[13]

In Lucille Clifton's memoir *Generations* (1976), her father Samuel Sayles, a tough steel mill worker in Buffalo, New York, and the "handsomest man in town," after tracing the family history of her name "Lucille" from his sister to his great-grandmother born in bondage, exclaims, "Oh slavery, slavery. . . . It ain't something in a book, Lue. Even the good parts was awful." On another occasion, however, he confides to Clifton, "We fooled em, Lue, slavery was terrible but we fooled them old people. We come out of it better than they did."[14] *Generations* stands as a literary enactment of the ceremonial West African oblation to the ancestors and the unborn. It pays homage to the women and men of an extended and blended African American family, descendants of "Dahomey people" from the same region William Craft once traversed, who remain close-knit and committed to each other in spite of interior struggles, forced or voluntary separations, and the daily humiliations and generational inequities first of slavery and then of Jim Crow.[15] By introducing each section of poetry before

Generations with epigraphs from Walt Whitman's American Renaissance masterpiece "Song of Myself" (1855), Clifton pays attention to what Timothy B. Powell describes as the "conflicting forces of inclusion and exclusion" that shaped both American literature and Americans' shifting notions of citizenship and community.[16] It is a book that insists on thinking about the history of African Americans as a transformative as well as traumatic one, and whose insistence on this diunital understanding of the African American past inspires my final reflection on what the Crafts' story may tell us about our remembrances of slavery.

Like the multigenerational family members of *Generations* who find themselves too often pitted against the bleakness of racism, poverty, and gender discrimination, the Crafts sustained themselves above it all because they faced their obstacles and disadvantages together. By alluding in public correspondence to the poet William Cowper's oft-quoted lines about former slaves only breathing free in England, the Crafts referenced the exhausting scenarios that prompted their escape in the first place.[17] Furthermore, they evoked their sensitivities about elevating themselves so that they might one day lift up others from the ranks of the impoverished and downtrodden. Theirs is a multivalent story that has proved alluring over the generations because it is not only one of oppression but also one of resistance and insurgency, a story that is effective precisely because they share one mind about freedom. As Tess Chakkalakal correctly explains in her study of themes of marriage and freedom in nineteenth-century antislavery fiction, "In the end, what made the story of William and Ellen Craft's escape from slavery so compelling for writers like Child, Stowe, and Brown was not just the transgressive means of their escape. It was their status as a *married* slave couple that made them into an instant sensation."[18]

They were not always side by side, of course. For example, during their journey from Georgia to the North, Ellen traveled in different railroad cars and slept in separate accommodations from those of William. Yet coming down to us side by side in spirit and resolve, they assure us that we too can bring our wildest, most sensational dreams to fruition. We are the lucky ones too, we who do not travel alone.

Notes

Introduction. The Crafts and the Memory of Slavery

1. Malcolm X Boulevard, otherwise known as Lenox Avenue, is one of many Harlem streets such as Adam Clayton Powell, Jr. Boulevard (Seventh Avenue) that have been co-named.

2. James.Baldwin, "The White Problem," 73, 77.

3. Zora Neale Hurston and Langston Hughes, *Mule Bone*, 10–11. See also Carla Kaplan, *Zora Neale Hurston*, 206–9, 214, 224.

4. The floor plan, appropriately entitled "Rivers," was conceived by artists Houston Conwill, Estella Conwill Majozo, and Joseph DePace. "Houston Conwill, Estella Conwill Majozo, and Joseph DePace," New York City Department of Cultural Affairs, http://www.nyc.gov/html/dcla/html/panyc/depace.shtml.

5. Patricia Hill Collins, *Black Feminist Thought*, 8–12; and Deborah King, "Multiple Jeopardy, Multiple Consciousness," 265–95.

6. A blend of "nigger" and "literati," Hurston's coinage poked fun at the social and intellectual pretensions of New Negroes, while saluting their bohemian attitudes and their offbeat opinions about art, creativity, and politics (Valerie Boyd, *Wrapped in Rainbows*, 116); Jessie Fauset, *Quicksand*, 80, 127.

7. Judith L. Stephens, *The Plays of Georgia Douglas Johnson*, 24.

8. Dorothy Sterling, "Ellen Craft: The Valiant Journey," in *Black Foremothers*, 3–59; and Richard J. M. Blackett, "The Odyssey of William and Ellen Craft," in *Beating against the Barriers*, 85–137.

9. Frances Smith Foster, "Creative Collaboration," 17.

10. Ezra Greenspan, *William Wells Brown*, xvi.

11. Waldo E. Martin Jr., *No Coward Soldiers*, 5.

12. Gerald McWorter, "The Nature and Needs of the Black University," 470–80.

13. JoyEllen Freeman, "A Portrayal of Power," 17–28.

14. Alice Walker, "Zora Neale Hurston," in *In Search of Our Mothers' Gardens*, 85, 91, 84, 86.

15. Gloria T. Hull and Barbara Smith, "Introduction," in *All the Women Are White, All the Blacks Are Men, but Some of Us Are Brave: Black Women's Studies*, ed. Gloria T. Hull, Patricia Bell Scott, and Barbara Smith (Old Westbury, NY: Feminist Press, 1982), xxvii.

16. Pier Gabrielle Foreman and Reginald H. Pitts, introduction to *Our Nig*, by Harriet E. Wilson, xxv.

17. RCA Victor records released Cooke's hit song and anthem "A Change is Gonna Come" posthumously in 1964, after he had been fatally shot by a hotel manager. Peter Guralnick, *Dream Boogie*, 546–54, 650–51; and Peter Guralnick, *Sweet Soul Music*.

18. Mark Twain, *The Adventures of Tom Sawyer*, 18, 51, 72.

19. See Donald B. Lemke, *The Brave Escape of William and Ellen Craft*.

20. Marlene D. Allen and Seretha D. Williams, *Afterimages of Slavery*, 2.

21. Robert Reid-Pharr, "The Post-Bellum Race Novel," 470–83.

22. Eric Gardner, *Unexpected Places*, 7.

23. Frances Smith Foster, "A Narrative," 735.

24. Ibid., 714, 715, 735, 723–25, 728–32. See also Eric Gardner, *Unexpected Places*, 7.

25. Elizabeth McHenry, *Forgotten Readers*; Eric Gardner, "Remembered (Black) Readers," 229–59; and Leon Jackson, "The Talking Book and the Talking Book Historian," 259–68.

26. Lois Brown, "Death-Defying Testimony," 132.

27. Ibid., 138. See also Armstrong, "A Mental and Moral Feast," 78–102.

28. Eric Gardner, class discussion, American Antiquarian Society, July 12, 2012.

29. Leon Jackson, "The Talking Book and the Talking Book Historian," 269.

30. In particular, the scholarly arguments about the visual iconography of Ellen Craft have been ongoing and generative. See, for example, Barbara McCaskill, "Yours Very Truly," 509–28; Ellen Weinauer, "A Most Respectable Looking Gentleman," 37–56; Lindon Barrett, "Hand-Writing, Legibility, and the White Body," 315–36; Ellen Samuels, "A Complication of Complaints," 15–47; P. Gabrielle Foreman, "Who's Your Mama?" 132–66; and Uri McMillan, "Ellen Craft's Radical Techniques of Subversion."

31. Beth A. McCoy, "Race and the (Para)textual Condition," 156.

32. Julia C. Collins, *The Curse of Caste*, xx.

Chapter One. The "Thrilling" Escape of William and Ellen Craft from Georgia

1. Jacqueline Goggin, *Carter G. Woodson*, 1–65; and Pellom McDaniels III, "The Prophetic Vision," 27, 35, 38–40. See also Darlene Clark Hine, "Carter G. Woodson," 405–8. My information about Woodson's extensive black history projects and publications also derives from a keynote address by the historians John Hope Franklin and Adelaide Cromwell, 91st Annual Convention of the Association for the Study of African American Life and History, Atlanta, Georgia, September 29, 2006.

2. Pero Gaglo Dagbovie, *The Early Black History Movement*, 55–60.

3. Carter Godwin Woodson, *Mind of the Negro*, 262–64; and Carter Godwin Woodson, "Letters to Antislavery Workers," 448.

4. Carter Godwin Woodson, "Thrilling Escape," 1. During World War II, USO clubs took out subscriptions to the *Bulletin* for black soldiers to read. Goggin, *Carter G. Woodson*, 114.

5. John Ernest, in *Running a Thousand Miles for Freedom*, 2000, xv–xvi.

6. Tritobia Hayes Benjamin, *Life and Art of Lois Mailou Jones*, 13–45; Charles H. Rowell, "Interview with Lois Mailou Jones," 359–62.

7. Carter Godwin Woodson, "Thrilling Escape," 1.

8. On January 1, 1863, President Abraham Lincoln (1809–65) emancipated the slaves in ten of the Confederate states that had not returned to the Union: Alabama, Arkansas, Florida, Georgia, Louisiana (not including twelve parishes already controlled by the Union), South Carolina, North Carolina, Mississippi, Texas, and Virginia. This did not include the border state of West Virginia and seven Virginia counties held by Grand Old Army forces.

9. William and Ellen Craft, *Running a Thousand Miles*, 1999, 7.

10. Norrece T. Jones Jr., "Rape in Black and White," 105.

11. William and Ellen Craft, *Running a Thousand Miles*, 1999, 3.

12. Ibid.; Kathryn Grover, *The Fugitive's Gibraltar*.

13. R. J. M. Blackett, "The Odyssey of William and Ellen Craft," in *Beating against the Barriers*, 86–137; Dorothy Sterling, "Ellen Craft: The Valiant Journey," in *Black Foremothers*, 3–59.

14. "Runaway Slaves," *Georgia Telegraph*, February 13, 1849.

15. James Olney, "I was Born," 152–53.

16. Jeffrey H. Richards, *Drama, Theatre, and Identity*, 232–33.

17. P. Gabrielle Foreman, "Who's Your Mama?," 524.

18. "The Libel Suit," 4; and William and Ellen Craft, *Running a Thousand Miles*, 1999, 8–11.

19. Donnie D. Bellamy, "Macon, Georgia," 298, 303; Allen D. Candler and Clement A. Evans, *Georgia*, 543.

20. In 1853, Eastburn's Press of Boston published a second edition of Collins's essay, perhaps to capitalize on the publicity and curiosity that had accompanied Collins's attempts to use the Fugitive Slave Law of 1850 to re-enslave the Crafts.

21. William and Ellen Craft, *Running a Thousand Miles*, 1999, 21; Berry, "*Swing the Sickle*," 35–45. See also the following for discussions of the kind of work that a nineteenth-century house slave and "ladies' maid" like Ellen Craft would be expected to do: Jacqueline Jones, *Labor of Love, Labor of Sorrow*; Dorothy Sterling, "Ellen Craft: The Valiant Journey," 8, 9–10; Brenda Stevenson, *Life in Black and White*; Deborah Gray White, *Ar'n't I a Woman?*, 62–91, 101–21; and David R. Goldfield, "Black Life in Old South Cities," 128, 138.

22. Dorothy Sterling, "Ellen Craft: The Valiant Journey," 10.

23. William and Ellen Craft, *Running a Thousand Miles*, 1999, 21.

24. Elizabeth Fox-Genovese, *Within the Plantation Household*, 34–35, 308–15.

25. Elredge J. McReady, "Wedding Feast in N.Y.," 1.

26. Dorothy Sterling, "Ellen Craft: The Valiant Journey," 6–7.

27. Brenda L. Stevenson, *Life in Black and White*, 228–29.

28. Armistead Wilson, in *Five Hundred Thousand Strokes for Freedom*, 5; William Wells Brown, "Singular Escape," 7; "William and Ellen Crafts[sic], The Fugitive Slaves from Boston," 6; "The Fugitive Slaves from Boston," 4.

29. Barbara McCaskill, "Yours Very Truly," 526, notes 2–4.

30. William and Ellen Craft, *Running a Thousand Miles*, 1999, 22, 53; and "The Libel Suit."

31. Steven Hahn, *A Nation under Our Feet*, 43; and class discussion with Hahn, W. E. B. Du Bois Institute, Harvard University, June 30, 2008.

32. Donnie D. Bellamy, "Macon, Georgia," 307.

33. Janet Cornelius Duitsman, *When I Can Read My Title Clear*, 5.

34. Steven Hahn, *A Nation under Our Feet*, 22.

35. "The Libel Suit."

36. *Five Hundred Thousand Strokes*, 5.

37. Steven Hahn, *A Nation under Our Feet*, 27.

38. Ibid., 41.

39. Major biographies of Parker are Weiss, *Life and Correspondence of Theodore Parker*; and Henry Steele Commager, *Theodore Parker*.

40. I am very grateful to Aghigh Ebrahimi Bazaz, formerly a research assistant for the Civil Rights Digital Library, for pointing out this usage by Dr. King in a sermon in Augusta, Georgia, on August 6, 1962, where he called for a "Second Emancipation Proclamation." Civil Rights Digital Library: Documenting America's Struggle for Racial Equality, http://crdl.usg.edu. Parker's original words read, "I do not pretend to understand the moral universe, the arc is a long one, my eye reaches but little ways; I cannot calculate the curve and complete the figure by the experience of sight; I can divine it by conscience. But from what I see I am sure it bends towards justice. Things refuse to be mismanaged long." Theodore Parker, "Of Justice and the Conscience," in *Ten Sermons of Religion*, 84–85.

41. Theodore Parker, *The Trial of Theodore Parker*, 146–47.

42. James Freeman Clarke, *Anti-Slavery Days*, 83–84.

43. John Ernest, "Representing Chaos: William Craft's *Running a Thousand Miles for Freedom*," *PMLA* 121, no. 2 (2006): 469–83.

44. I am very appreciative to Katherine E. Flynn for sharing with me her discovery of the Massachusetts death record for Mary Elizabeth Craft. She is listed as having died in on January 23, 1870, of "Pleuro Pneumonia at the age of 1 year 3 months and 27 days." Katherine E. Flynn to Barbara McCaskill, email, May 23, 2006, and October 6, 2008.

45. See, for example, George W. Clark, "Appalling Features of Slavery," in *The Liberty Minstrel*, 1–2; and Charlotte Elizabeth, "The Slave and Her Babe," in Clark, *The Liberty Minstrel*, 13.

46. See also Frances Ellen Watkins Harper's "The Slave Mother," in Frances Smith Foster, *A Brighter Coming Day*, 58–59; "The Blind Slave Boy" in William Wells

Brown, *Anti-Slavery Harp*, 7; and Harriet Beecher Stowe's chapters "The Mother's Struggle" and "Eliza's Escape" of her *Uncle Tom's Cabin*, 44–70. For a detailed analysis of the cross-pollination of styles, ideas, and arguments among nineteenth-century British and American abolitionists, see Valerie Domenica Levy, *The Antislavery Web of Connection*.

47. John Sekora, "Black Message/White Envelope," 482–515.

48. Jeffrey Ruggles, *The Unboxing of Henry Box Brown*, 27–32.

49. John Eisenberg, *The Great Match Race*, 187–97; "Intersectional Match Races," International Museum of the Horse.

Chapter Two. Boston's Glorious Fugitives

1. Archibald H. Grimké, "Anti-Slavery Boston," 458; Allen Chamberlain, *Beacon Hill*, 221; Robert C. Hayden and the staff of the Museum of Afro-American History, *The African Meeting House in Boston*, 18–25; Thomas O'Connor, *Eminent Bostonians*, 133–34; Jaci Conry, "The Other Beacon Hill," 66.

2. James Oliver Horton and Lois E. Horton, *Black Bostonians*, 55.

3. Gary Collison, *Shadrach Minkins*, 64.

4. Robert C. Hayden, *African Americans in Boston*, 76–77, 104; Jaci Conry, "The Other Beacon Hill," 62, 63–64; James Oliver Horton and Lois E. Horton, *Black Bostonians*, 8–10, 102–03; "Black Occupations and Social Stratification," Boston African American National Historic Site, http://www.nps.gov/boaf/index.htm.

5. Lewis Hayden, advertisement, *The Liberator*, July 13, 1849, 111; William Craft, advertisement, *The Liberator*, July 27, 1849, 119.

6. Sarah Meer, *Uncle Tom Mania*, 189; Gay Gibson Cima, *Performing Anti-Slavery*, 191, 196–207.

7. See, for example, "Runaway Slaves," *Georgia Telegraph and Messenger* (Macon), February 13, 1849; Lyman Allen, "William and Ellen Craft," *The Liberator*, March 2, 1849, 35; "Welcome to the Fugitives," *The Liberator*, April 6, 1849, 54.

8. Fergus M. Bordewitch, *Bound for Canaan*, 309.

9. Deborah Willis, *Reflections in Black*, 4, 5.

10. Pamela Hoyle, *Development of Photography in Boston*, 6, 8–11.

11. David Tatham, *Winslow Homer and the Pictorial Press*, 19–47.

12. Nell Irvin Painter, *Sojourner Truth*, 196.

13. Kim Sichel, *Black Boston*; Gwendolyn DuBois Shaw, "Landscapes of Labor," 59–73.

14. Gwendolyn DuBois Shaw, *Portraits of a People*, 13.

15. Deborah Willis, "The Sociologist's Eye," 51–78.

16. Frederick Douglass, "Negro Portraits," 18.

17. Gwendolyn DuBois Shaw, *Portraits of a People*, 14.

18. Ann Fabian, *The Unvarnished Truth*, 80.

19. Marcus Wood, *Blind Memory*, 78–142.

20. Teresa C. Zackodnik, *The Mulatta and the Politics of Race*, 58.

21. See Jerome Farrell, "Ellen Craft (1825/6–91)," *Oxford Dictionary of National*

Biography, http://www.oxforddnb.com/index/46/101046318; and Jeffrey Green, "A Black Family in Rural Surrey in the 1850s," http://www.jeffreygreen.co.uk/059-a -black-family-in-rural-surrey-in-the-1850s.

22. See *The Fourth Exhibition of the Massachusetts Charitable Mechanic Association*, 25; *The Fifth Exhibition of the Massachusetts Charitable Mechanic Association*, 24; *The Sixth Exhibition of the Massachusetts Charitable Mechanic Association*, 147; *The Seventh Exhibition of the Massachusetts Charitable Mechanic Association*, 103, 105.

23. Ronald Polito, *A Directory of Boston Photographers*, 37; *The Boston Directory*, 61, 151, 323; *Directory of the City of Boston*, 77, 176, 285. See also "Hale, Luther Holman" in Craig, *Craig's Daguerreian Registry*.

24. Ann Fabian, *The Unvarnished Truth*, 85.

25. Teresa C. Zackodnick, *The Mulatta and the Politics of Race*, 43–50.

26. Eric Lott, *Love and Theft*, 15–62.

27. For discussions of Webb's performances of Stowe's *Christian Slave*, see Meer, *Uncle Tom Mania*, 185–93; and Eric Gardner, *Major Voices*, 259–64.

28. Carolyn L. Karcher, *The First Woman of the Republic*; Gardner, *Major Voices*, 441–42.

29. William Wells Brown, *The Escape*, 3.

30. Valerie Domenica Levy, The Antislavery Web of Connection.

31. *The Stars and Stripes* cited in Gardner, *Major Voices*, 468, 445, 452, 465, 466, 468.

32. Ibid., 455.

33. Ibid., 458, 461, 459–61, 460.

34. Ibid., 456, 457.

35. Ibid., 445. For the full text of "Adams and Liberty," written in 1798 by the son of the patriot Thomas Paine, see Robert Treat Paine, *Works*, 245–47.

36. William's quatrain is a variation of the final stanza from Mary Collier's antislavery poem "Fourth of July": "Say to the captive toiling / In freedom's proud abode, / "Cast off thy fetter, brother, / Take back the *gift of God*." / Let not oppression linger / Where starry banners wave; / Swell high the shout of freedom / Let it echo for the slave." Maria Weston Chapman, *Songs of the Free*, 103–05.

37. Eric Gardner, *Major Voices*, 446.

38. Ibid., 475.

39. William Cowper, *The Task and Other Poems*, 36.

40. Eric Gardner. *Major Voices*, 461, 465, 471.

41. Stowe, *Uncle Tom's Cabin*, 348–53.

42. Hannah Crafts, *The Bondwoman's Narrative*, xxxv, 83–87. According to Greg Hecimovitch, Bond was enslaved on a North Carolina plantation. After escaping in 1857, she published her novel. Julie Bosman, "Professor Says He Has Solved a Mystery," A3.

43. In chapter 19, the novel's light-skinned heroine Clotel decides to masquerade as a white man in her bid for freedom, accompanied by another slave, named William, who has agreed to pose as her servant. William Wells Brown, *Clotel*, 2000, 164–77. For a discussion of Brown's traveling panorama, see Daphne A. Brooks, *Bodies in Dissent*, 81–84; and Jeffrey Ruggles, *The Unboxing of Henry Brown*, 69–110, 119–38.

44. James Oliver Horton and Lois E. Horton, *Black Bostonians*, 102; Betty De-Ramus, *Forbidden Fruit*, 50–51.

45. William and Ellen Craft, *Running a Thousand Miles for Freedom*, 1999, 54, 65, 66.

46. Ibid., 54.

47. James Oliver Horton and Lois E. Horton, *Black Bostonians*, 66.

48. Among the many sources on this slave chase, see "Slave Hunters Arrested," *Georgia Telegraph and Messenger* (Macon) November 5, 1850; "The Fugitive Slave Case in Boston," *Georgia Telegraph and Messenger*, November 6, 1850; "The Boston Slave Hunt and the Vigilance Committee," *Georgia Telegraph and Messenger*, November 12, 1850; *Liverpool Mercury*, November 12, 1850; "The Boston Excitement," *Georgia Telegraph and Messenger*, November 13, 1850; *Report of the Great Antislavery Meeting*, 11–12; "The Boston Slave Hunt," *New York Tribune*, December 9, 1850, 5; "The Slave Hunt in Boston," *The (Boston) Commonwealth*, January 15, 1851; Vincent Y. Bowditch, *Life and Correspondence*, 372.

49. "Theodore Parker," *The Liberator*, October 7, 1864, 164.

50. Lois Brown, "Death-Defying Testimony," 132. For excellent analytical discussions of African American literature and culture based on public documents, periodical sources, and printing records, see Lara Langer Cohen and Jordan Stein, eds., *Early African American Print Culture* (Philadelphia: University of Pennsylvania Press, 2012).

51. 1851 marriage registry, City of Boston, Massachusetts Archives.

52. Letters from George W. Putnam of Lynn, Massachusetts, to Wilbur H. Siebert (November 5, 1893 and December 27, 1893) and letter from David Mead of Saugus, Massachusetts, to Wilbur H. Siebert (March 1893). In the Wilbur H. Siebert collection relating to the Underground Railroad and fugitive slaves, circa 1891–98, scrapbooks of *The Underground Railroad in Massachusetts Vol. 2*, container 14, Houghton Library, Harvard College Library, Harvard University. See also Wilbur H. Siebert, *The Underground Railroad from Slavery to Freedom*, 132–33, 252; Wilbur H. Siebert, *The Underground Railroad in Massachusetts*, 42–43; Priscilla Sawyer Lord and Virginia Clegg Gamage, *Marblehead*, 172, 173; "Poets, Shoemakers, and Freedom Seekers," 4, http://www.nps.gov/sama/historyculture/upload/ugrrsm.pdf.

53. Robin W. Winks, *The Blacks in Canada*.

54. Bridglal Pachai and Henry Bishop, *Historic Black Nova Scotia*, 1–6. African Genealogical Society, *The Spirit of Africville*, 106–13.

55. "African Canadians and the War of 1812," symposium, Black Cultural Centre for Nova Scotia, Cherry Brook, Nova Scotia, November 23–24, 2012.

56. William and Ellen Craft, *Running a Thousand Miles*, 199, 66. The Crafts credit a Rev. Cannady and his wife for offering them a place to stay, but this may very likely be a misspelling of "Kennedy." In 1850, the Rev. Hugh Kennedy was a minister of the A.M.E. Zion Church (founded 1846) at the corner of Gottingen and Falkland Streets in Halifax. David W. States to Barbara McCaskill, email, Dec. 10, 2012.

57. *Belcher's Farmer's Almanack* (Halifax, Nova Scotia: C. H. Belcher, 1824–68).

58. Stephen Fox, *Transatlantic*, 112, 113.

59. Ibid., 113.

60. Ibid., 200.

61. William and Ellen Craft, *Running a Thousand Miles for Freedom*, 1999, 66.

62. Timetable, British and North American Royal Mail Steam-Ships, *Liverpool Mercury*, November 1, 1850, 4; "Arrival of the British and North American Royal Mail Steam-Ship, Cambria," *Liverpool Mercury*, December 13, 1850, 2.

63. Gretchen Holbrook Gerzina, *Black Victorians, Black Victoriana*; and Gretchen Holbrook Gerzina, *Black London: Life before Emancipation*.

Chapter Three. Running a Thousand Miles in England

1. In his biography of Douglass, William S. McFeely writes that he was "denied a cabin on the *Cambria*" and traveled in steerage with the American abolitionist James Buffum. William S. McFeely, *Frederick Douglass* (New York: W. W. Norton, 1991), 120.

2. As I write in my introductory essay to the University of Georgia Press's edition of *Running a Thousand Miles for Freedom*, nineteenth-century antislavery and sentimental writers such as Frances Ellen Watkins Harper and Lydia Maria Child frequently evoked the phrase "pleasant homes" in their critiques of southern slavery. McCaskill, introduction to *Running a Thousand Miles for Freedom*, by William and Ellen Craft (Athens: University of Georgia Press, 1999), ix, note 4.

3. Early scholarship on *Running a Thousand Miles for Freedom* discussed it as a single-authored work written by William. Since the 1990s, as I write in the my introduction to this book, many researchers, including myself, have challenged this claim—most recently, Geoffrey Sanborn, who attributes portions of the Crafts' narrative to William Wells Brown. Although William tells their history from a first-person perspective, I refer to the memoir as a co-authored text to acknowledge Ellen's contributions to shaping their story on the antislavery stage as well as possibly on paper.

4. Ernest, "Representing Chaos," 479.

5. William and Ellen Craft, *Running a Thousand Miles for Freedom*, 1999, 66; and Jeffrey Green to Barbara McCaskill, email, Aug. 1, 2012.

6. For discussions of Liverpool's role in the transatlantic slave trade, see Anthony Tibbles, ed., *Transatlantic Slavery: Against Human Dignity* (London: HMSO, 1994); James Walvin, *Black Ivory: A History of British Slavery* (London: Fontana Press, 1993); Gail Cameron and Stan Crook, *Liverpool: Capital of the Slave Trade* (Rockland, Me.: Picton Press, 1992); and Roger Anstey and P. E. H. Hair, eds., *Liverpool, the African Slave Trade, and Abolition: Essays to Illustrate Current Knowledge and Research*, enlarged ed. (Liverpool: Historic Society of Lancashire and Cheshire, 1989).

7. William and Ellen Craft, *Running a Thousand Miles for Freedom*, 1999, 58.

8. I am grateful to Rhondda Robinson Thomas and Martha Pitts for pointing out these texts to me.

9. Gerald L. Early, "The End of Race as We Know It."

10. Frances Smith Foster, introduction to *Witnessing Slavery*, xxi.

11. Deborah Gray White, *Ar'n't I a Woman? Female Slaves in the Plantation South* (1985; reprint, New York: W. W. Norton, 1987), 76.

12. Philip Gould, "The Rise, Development, and Circulation of the Slave Narrative," in *The Cambridge Companion to the African American Slave Narrative*, edited by Audrey A. Fisch (Cambridge, UK: Cambridge University Press, 2007), 19.

13. William and Ellen Craft *Running a Thousand Miles for Freedom*, 1999, 3, 8.

14. Ibid., 3, 8.

15. The historian John Bailey situates the story of the kidnapped five-year-old Salomé Müller, who became known by a variety of English names, within nineteenth-century attitudes toward race and immigration. Casting doubt on her whiteness, and carefully examining both testimonies and silences in the legal drama that revolved around her, he contends that Müller actually was a slave who seized the chance of a lifetime to be free. Carol Wilson also examines legal documentation of the case to raise questions about the veracity of Müller's claims and the validity of perceived racial and social categories. John Bailey, *The Lost German Slave Girl: The Extraordinary True Story of Sally Miller and Her Fight for Freedom in Old New Orleans* (New York: Atlantic Monthly Press, 2003); and Carol Wilson, *The Two Lives of Sally Miller: A Case of Mistaken Identity in Antebellum New Orleans* (New Brunswick, N.J.: Rutgers University Press, 2007).

16. Louisa Picquet, *Louisia Picquet: The Octoroon: A Tale of Southern Slave Life*, in *Collected Black Women's Narratives*, introduction by Anthony G. Barthelemy (1861; repr., New York: Oxford University Press, 1988), 48. *The Octoroon* was first published in 1861.

17. William and Ellen Craft, *Running a Thousand Miles for Freedom*, 1999, 9, 10.

18. "Slavery," *The Newcastle Courant*, Dec. 4, 1857.

19. William and Ellen Craft, *Running a Thousand Miles for Freedom*, 1999, 10.

20. William and Ellen Craft, *Running a Thousand Miles for Freedom*, 1999, 12.

21. *Anti-Slavery Reporter* (London), June 1, 1860: 143.

22. Geoffrey Sanborn, "The Plagiarist's Craft: Fugitivity and Theatricality in *Running a Thousand Miles for Freedom*," *PMLA* 128, no. 4 (2013): 907–22.

23. *Newcastle Courant*, December 15, 1865.

24. "Ellen Craft and Her Mother," *American Anti-Slavery Standard*, August 12, 1865.

25. Heather Andrea Williams, *Help Me to Find My People: The African American Search for Family Lost in Slavery* (Chapel Hill: University of North Carolina Press, 2012), 156.

26. William and Ellen Craft, *Running a Thousand Miles for Freedom*, 1999, 38, 45.

27. *Newcastle Courant*, December 15, 1865.

28. Eric Gardner, "'This Attempt of Their Sister': Harriet Wilson's *Our Nig* from Printer to Readers," *New England Quarterly* 66, no. 2 (June 1993): 226–46.

29. William and Ellen Craft, *Running a Thousand Miles for Freedom*, 1999, 3.

30. Frederick Douglass, *Narrative of the Life of Frederick Douglass, an American Slave*, in *Shadowing Slavery: Five African American Autobiographical Narratives*, edited by John Ernest (1845; reprint, Acton, Mass.: Copley, 2002), 23, 28, 37.

31. William Wells Brown, *Narrative of William W. Brown, A Fugitive Slave*, in *From Fugitive Slave to Free Man: The Autobiographies of William Wells Brown*, edited by William L. Andrews (1848; reprint, New York: Penguin, 1993), 28, 34.

32. Harriet A. Jacobs, *Incidents in the Life of a Slave Girl*, 5.

33. Gould, "The Rise, Development, and Circulation of the Slave Narrative," 19.

34. Tess Chakkalakal, *Novel Bondage*; and Frances Smith Foster, *'Til Death and Distance*.

35. Robert Collins, *Essay on the Treatment and Management of Slaves*.

36. "William and Ellen Crafts [*sic*]." *Christian Watchman and Reflector*, June 19, 1851, 99.

37. "The President's Letter to Dr. Collins, the Owner of Crafts [*sic*]," *New York Herald*, November 20, 1850, 1, 99.

38. See my discussion of William and Ellen's public letter to antislavery friends published in November 1851, in McCaskill, "Yours Very Truly," 521–23, 525–26.

39. Jean Fagan Yellin, introduction to *Incidents in the Life of a Slave Girl*, by Harriet A. Jacobs, enlarged ed. (1861; reprint, Cambridge, Mass.: Harvard University Press, 2000), xxix, xxx.

40. This businessman and Underground Railroad conductor also greeted the fugitive Henry "Box" Brown who famously escaped from Richmond, Virginia, to Philadelphia when colleagues shipped him in a box. See Jeffrey Ruggles, *The Unboxing of Henry Brown*. William and Ellen Craft, *Running a Thousand Miles for Freedom*, 1999, 66.

41. William and Ellen Craft, *Running a Thousand Miles for Freedom*, 1999, 66.

42. The Crafts reprint this letter in *Running a Thousand Miles for Freedom*, 1999, 55–7.

43. William and Ellen Craft, *Running a Thousand Miles for Freedom*, 1999, 57, 67.

44. William and Ellen Craft, *Running a Thousand Miles for Freedom*, 1999, 58.

45. Ernest, "Representing Chaos," 474.

46. William and Ellen Craft, *Running a Thousand Miles for Freedom*, 1999, 58. The memoir does identify "Mr. Barkley Ivens and his dear family," the Quaker farmer and family who invite them to stay at their home after the Crafts have arrived in the North, as incomparable and peerless among their "very kind and hospitable friends, in American and England." "We have never been under a roof where we have been made to feel more at home," writes William, "or where the inmates took a deeper interest in our well-being." *Running a Thousand Miles for Freedom*, 1999, 54. My conjecture is that the Ivenses are singled out for this gratitude not only because they were the first family the Crafts resided with in freedom, but also because of the extensive involvement of the Society of Friends throughout their lives. Quakers, for example, pledged significant funds toward William's travels to West Africa in the 1860s. William is careful not to heap praise upon these initial allies without also recognizing the transatlantic community of activists to which he and Ellen now claim membership.

47. William and Ellen Craft, *Running a Thousand Miles for Freedom*, 1999, 64–66, 69.

48. William and Ellen Craft, *Running a Thousand Miles for Freedom*, 1999, 62, 66, 67. John Ernest, "Representing Chaos," 481.

49. William and Ellen Craft, *Running a Thousand Miles for Freedom*, 1999, 55, 56, 57.

50. William and Ellen Craft, *Running a Thousand Miles for Freedom*, 1999, 54–57.

51. William and Ellen Craft, *Running a Thousand Miles for Freedom*, 1999, 47.

52. Benedict Anderson, *Imagined Communities*.

53. William and Ellen Craft, *Running a Thousand Miles for Freedom*, 1999, 21, 27, 28.

54. Henry Brown (1815–ca. 1879) escaped bondage in Richmond, Virginia, in 1849 by enlisting friends to seal him in a wooden box and ship him by various conveyances to Philadelphia. In the 1850s, he exhibited both the box and an antislavery panorama entitled "The Mirror of Slavery" throughout the northern United States and Great Britain. After he unsuccessfully attempted to help a group of enslaved Africans escape Florida on his boat in 1844, Jonathan Walker (1799–1878) was branded with an "SS" (for "slave stealer") on his right hand. See Daphne A. Brooks, *Bodies in Dissent*, 66–130; and Marcus Wood, *Blind Memory*, 243, 246–50.

55. HollyGale Millette, "Exchanging Fugitive Identity: William and Ellen Craft's Transatlantic Reinvention (1850–69)," in *Imagining Transatlantic Slavery*, edited by Cara Kaplan and John Oldfield (Houndmills, UK: Palgrave Macmillan, 2010), 69.

56. William and Ellen Craft, *Running a Thousand Miles for Freedom*, 1999, 26.

57. "A righteous man regardeth the life of his beast; but the tender mercies of the wicked are cruel" (Proverbs 12:10). William and Ellen Craft, *Running a Thousand Miles for Freedom*, 1999, 68.

58. William's key rhymes with Ellen's concealment, prior to their departure, of the clothing he has purchased and she has sewn for her planter's disguise. "[A]mongst other pieces of furniture which I had made in my overtime," writes William, who is hired out in service by his master in service as a carpenter, "was a chest of drawers; so when I took the articles home, she locked them up carefully in these drawers. No one about the premises knew she had anything of the kind." William and Ellen Craft, *Running a Thousand Miles for Freedom*, 1999, 21, 28, 50. Additionally, Daneen Wardrop presents an excellent analysis of William's key as a gendered symbol of his power and visibility as coauthor (with Ellen) of their narrative in "Collaboration in *Running a Thousand Miles for Freedom*: William's Key and Ellen's Renaming," *Arizona Quarterly*, vol. 61, no. 3 (Autumn 2005): 57–73.

59. William and Ellen Craft, *Running a Thousand Miles for Freedom*, 1999, 54. "[T]he father of the slave may be the President of the Republic; but if the mother should be a slave at the infant's birth, the poor child is ever legally doomed to the same fate." Ibid., 12. This quotation references *Clotel* (1852), the best-selling novel of William Wells Brown and the oldest-known published novel by an African American. According to Brown's biographer Ezra Greenspan, "Brown took the subject of the novel, the lives of the illegitimate, mixed-race, slave daughters and granddaughters of Thomas Jefferson, from rumors widely disseminated in his day." Ezra Greenspan, "Writing African American Fiction," in his *William Wells Brown: A Reader*, 173. Greenspan, *William Wells Brown: A Reader*, 163n58.

60. *Bristol Mercury*, August 30, 1851.

61. *Aberdeen Journal*, February 12, 1851; *Bristol Mercury*, April 26, 1851.

62. "American Slavery," *Leeds Mercury*, October 23, 1856; "Fugitive Slaves from the United States, *Bristol Mercury*, Nov. 30, 1850.

63. Lydia Maria Child, "William and Ellen Crafts [*sic*]," in Child, *Freedmen's Book*, iii, 179–204.

64. "Mr. William Craft's Mission to Dahomey," *Newcastle Courant*, July 1, 1864.

65. Child, *Freedmen's Book*, 199, 202, 269. Unfortunately, William's trade left him in debt and forced him to sell the family's home in 1867. Jean Fagan Yellin, *Harriet Jacobs: A Life*, 214.

66. Child, *Freedmen's Book*, 202.

67. *American Slavery: Report of the Great Anti-Slavery Meeting*, 7–8.

68. Five years later, British antislavery audiences would observe a more composed and fluent William Craft. Inviting the public to attend an antislavery lecture where he was the featured speaker, the *Leeds Mercury* stated, "We may say that, though of African blood and bred in servitude, he speaks with the facility and accuracy of an English gentleman." "American Slavery.—Escape of William and Ellen Craft," *Leeds Mercury*, October 23, 1856.

69. "Mr. Craft's Mission to Dahomey," *Caledonian Mercury*, July 3, 1863.

70. Ibid.

71. Ibid.

Chapter Four. The Boston Libel Trial of William Craft

1. "The Craft-Naylor Suit," 2; Buddy Sullivan, "Black Education in Bryan"; Charles and Tess Hoffman, *North by South*; *Craft v. Schlesinger, et al.* (April term 1878, case no. 1752), Massachusetts Supreme Judicial Court Archives.

2. "Mr. William Craft's Mission to Dahomey."

3. William Craft, "Primary Education in Georgia."

4. "The Feeling in the South."

5. "The Libel Suit," 2; Jenifer L. Barclay, "Coming Full Circle," 169–70.

6. William Craft initially partnered with a white man named Charles Delamotte in leasing and then purchasing Woodville, with the understanding that Craft would assume management of the farm and Delamotte would oversee financial and legal affairs in Savannah. The partnership dissolved, however, and William lost considerable money settling with Delamotte. "The Craft-Naylor Suit"; William Craft, "Primary Education in Georgia."

7. *Boston Daily Advertiser*, August 22, 1873, 2; and June 8, 1878, 2.

8. *Boston Daily Advertiser*, June 8, 1878, 2; "Craft v. Schlesinger," 4.

9. The defendants in the tort were Sebastian B. Schlesinger, B. Schlesinger, and George P. King, all of whom were members of Naylor and Company, along with a clerk in the company recorded as William Clark. "The Libel Suit."

10. "A Notable Case," 2.

11. See the following issues of the 1878 *Boston Daily Advertiser*: June 6–8, June 14, June 16.

12. Harriet E. Wilson, *Our Nig*, 127, 128. In *The Fugitive's Gibraltar* (197–98), Kathryn Grover also mentions suspected cases of such fraud in mid-nineteenth-century New Bedford, Massachusetts.

13. *Boston Daily Advertiser*, June 14, 1878, 2. The phrase "thousands of millions" suggests the biblical lines "And they blessed Rebekah, and said unto her, Thou art our sister, be thou the mother of thousands of millions, and let thy seed possess the gate of those which hate them" (Gen. 24:60).

14. "It is interesting to note," Millette adds, "that after arriving in Philadelphia they moved directly to Boston—two cities that would emerge as the centre of the black aristocracy." HollyGale Millette, "Exchanging Fugitive Identity," 64, 67.

15. Carole Emberton, "It's (Still) a Man's World: Gendering Freedom in the Civil War Era," public lecture, Miller Learning Center, University of Georgia, Athens, Oct. 23, 2013.

16. "The Craft Libel Suit."

17. Ibid.

18. Ibid.

19. Ibid.

20. "The Libel Suit."

21. "Mr. William Craft and His School," *Boston Daily Advertiser*, Oct. 4, 1876.

22. "The Craft Libel Suit."

23. William Still, *The Underground Rail Road*, 3.

24. W. E. B. Du Bois, *The Philadelphia Negro*. Similarly, Lonnie Bunch, director of the National Museum of African American History and Culture, has named William and Ellen Craft among many examples of black ancestors whose stories inspire and guide contemporary Americans to face challenges and transform society. Lonnie Bunch, "Knowing the Past Opens the Door to the Future," in "Our American Story," Smithsonian Institution, National Museum of African American History and Culture, http://go.si.edu/site/PageServer?pagename=%2Fmm_stories#bhm.

25. "William Craft."

26. Lydia Maria Child, *The Freedmen's Book*, 204.

Epilogue. A Story to Pass Down

1. Caroline Gebhard to Barbara McCaskill, email, May 24, 2002.

2. "Craft, Henry Kempton," in *Who's Who in Colored America: A Biographical Dictionary of Notable Living Persons of African Descent in America, 1930–1931–1932* (Brooklyn, N.Y.: T. Yenser, 1933), 111; and Lynn Hamilton, "The Story of a Quest to Be Free," Philly.com, http://articles.philly.com/1991-02-17/news/25774516_1_ellen-craft-william-craft-freedom.

3. Lynn Hamilton, "The Story of a Quest to Be Free," Philly.com.

4. See Stephen R. Fox, *The Guardian of Boston: William Monroe Trotter* (New York: Atheneum, 1970).

5. For Keckley: Yellin, *Harriet Jacobs*, 162.

6. Tom Burham, *The Dictionary of Misinformation* (New York: Cornhill, 1975), 258–59.

7. Rafia Zafar, *We Wear the Mask*, 87.

8. Toni Morrison, *Beloved: A Novel* (New York: Knopf, 1987), 210, 211.

9. John Hope Franklin and Alfred A. Moss Jr., *From Slavery to Freedom*, 8th ed., 49.

10. See Michael A. Gomez, *Exchanging Our Country Marks: The Transformation of African Identities in the Colonial and Antebellum South* (Chapel Hill: University of North Carolina Press, 1998); and Robert Farris Thompson, *Flash of the Spirit: African & Afro-American Art and Philosophy* (New York: Random House, 1983).

11. Katrina Browne, Alla Kovgan, and Jude Ray, *Traces of the Trade: A Story from the Deep North* (San Francisco: California Newsreel, 2008); Debra Goldschmidt, "Colleges Come to Terms with Slave-Owning Pasts"; Craig Steven Wilder, *Ebony and Ivy: Race, Slavery and the Troubled History of America's Universities* (New York: Bloomsbury Press, 2013). In February 2011, Emory University hosted "Slavery and the University: Histories and Legacies," a scholarly conference designed to share research and encourage initiatives and partnerships exploring this theme.

12. Eric Gardner, *Unexpected Places*, 6, 7–8, 10, 12, 13–14.

13. Laurie F. Maffly-Kipp, *Setting Down the Sacred Past*, 201–33; John Ernest, *Liberation Historiography*, 276–329; Rhondda Robinson Thomas, *Claiming Exodus*, 1–7.

14. Clifton, "Generations," in *Good Woman*, 237, 260. First published as *Generations: A Memoir* (New York: Random House, 1976).

15. Ibid., 260.

16. Lucille Clifton, *Good Woman*; Timothy B. Powell, *Ruthless Democracy*, 12.

17. The full quotation, from Cowper's multivolume poem *The Task* (2.40–42) reads, "Slaves cannot breathe in England: if their lungs / Receive our air, that moment they are free; / They touch our country, and their shackles fall." McCaskill, "Yours Very Truly," 527n8.

18. Tess Chakkalakal, *Novel Bondage*, 9.

Bibliography

Manuscripts and Archives

Arthur and Elizabeth Schlesinger Library on the History of Women in America, Radcliffe Institute for Advanced Study, Harvard University
Avery Research Center for African American History and Culture, College of Charleston
Boston Athenæum
Boston Public Library Anti-Slavery Collection, Rare Books and Manuscript Library
Georgia Historical Society
Hargrett Rare Book and Manuscript Library, University of Georgia
Harvard University Archives
Houghton Library, Harvard College Library, Harvard University
Library Company of Philadelphia
Massachusetts Archives
Massachusetts Historical Society
Massachusetts Supreme Judicial Court Archives
Middle Georgia Archives, Washington Memorial Library, Macon
Nova Scotia Archives
Samuel J. May Anti-Slavery Collection, Cornell University
Schomburg Center for Research in Black Culture / New York Public Library
University of California, Berkeley, Bancroft Library

Historical Newspapers and Periodicals

Aberdeen Journal and General Advertiser for the North of Scotland, 1797–1896
Anti-Slavery Advocate (London), 1852–63

Anti-Slavery Reporter, 1853

Boston Daily Advertiser, 1836–1921

Boston Evening Journal, 1872–98

Bristol Mercury, 1819–1900

Caledonian Mercury (Edinburgh, Scotland), 1720–1867

Christian Union (New York), 1870–93

Christian Watchman and Reflector (Boston), 1851–66

Commonwealth (Boston), 1862–80

Freed-Man (London), 1865–68

Georgia Journal and Messenger (Macon), 1847–69

Georgia Telegraph (Macon), 1844–58

Glasgow Herald, 1805–1902

Illustrated London News, 1842–2003

Indianapolis Sentinel, 1880–1904

Leeds Mercury, 1807–1901

Liberator (Boston), 1831–65

Liberty Bell (Boston), 1843–58

Liverpool Mercury, and Lancashire, Cheshire and General Advertiser, 1847–1904

London Morning Chronicle, 1789–1865

National Anti-Slavery Standard (New York), 1840–70

Negro History Bulletin (Washington, D.C.), 1937–2001

Newcastle Courant, 1711–1884

New York Herald, 1840–1920

New York Tribune, 1866–1924

North Star (Rochester, N.Y.), 1847–51

Pennsylvania Freeman, 1838–54

Provincial Freeman (Windsor, Toronto, and Chatham, Ontario), 1853–57

Young England: An Illustrated Magazine for Boys throughout the English-Speaking World (London), 1880–1937

Online Sources

"American Eclipse." *Unofficial Thoroughbred Hall of Fame*. http://www.spiletta.com /UTHOF/ameclipse.html.

"The Autobiography of Malcolm X." *American Icons: A Radio Series from Studio 360*. http://www.studio360.org/2011/aug/26.

Bible: King James Version. University of Michigan Library Digital Collection. http:// quod.lib.umich.edu/k/kjv.

Boston African American National Historic Site. http://www.nps.gov/boaf/index .htm.

Bunch, Lonnie. "Knowing the Past Opens the Door to the Future." In "Our American Story," Smithsonian Institution, National Museum of African American History and Culture. http://go.si.edu/site/PageServer?pagename=%2Fmm_stories# bhm.

Civil Rights Digital Library: Documenting America's Struggle for Racial Equality. http://crdl.usg.edu.

Farrell, Jerome. "Ellen Craft (1825/6–1891)." *Oxford Dictionary of National Biography*. Oxford University Press, 2011. First published 2004. http://www.oxforddnb.com /view/article/46318.

———. "William Craft (c. 1825–1900)." *Oxford Dictionary of National Biography*. Oxford University Press, 2004. http://www.oxforddnb.com/view/article/46317/.

Green, Jeffrey. "A Black Family in Rural Surrey in the 1850s." http://www.jeffreygreen .co.uk/059-a-black-family-in-rural-surrey-in-the-1850s.

"Houston Conwill, Estella Conwill Majozo, and Joseph DePace." New York City Department of Cultural Affairs. http://www.nyc.gov/html/dcla/html/panyc /depace.shtml.

"Intersectional Match Races." International Museum of the Horse. http://imh.org /exhibits/online/intersectional-match-races.

Leslie, Kent Anderson. "Lucy Craft Laney (1854–1933)." *The New Georgia Encyclopedia*. http://www.georgiaencyclopedia.org/articles/education/lucy-craft-laney -1854-1933.

"Poets, Shoemakers, and Freedom Seekers: Abolitionists and the Underground Railroad in Essex County." National Park Service. U.S. Department of Interior, and Salem Maritime National Historic Site, Salem, Massachusetts. http://www.nps .gov/sama/historyculture/upload/ugrrsm.pdf.

Published Sources

Africville Genealogical Society. *The Spirit of Africville*. Halifax, N.S.: Formac, 2010.

Allen, Marlene D., and Seretha D. Williams, eds. *Afterimages of Slavery: Essays on Appearances in Recent American Films, Literature, Television, and Other Media*. Jefferson, N.C.: McFarland, 2012.

American Slavery: Report of the Great Anti-Slavery Meeting Held April 9, 1851, in the Public Room, Broadmead, Bristol, to Receive the Fugitive Slaves, William and Ellen Craft. Bristol, UK: James Ackland, 1851.

Ampadu, Lena. "Maria W. Stewart and the Rhetoric of Black Preaching." In *Black Women's Intellectual Traditions*, edited by Kristin Waters and Carol B. Conaway, 38–54. Burlington: University of Vermont Press, 2007.

Anderson, Benedict. *Imagined Communities: Reflections on the Origin and Spread of Nationalism*. Rev. ed. London: Verso, 2006.

Anderson, John. *The Story of the Life of John Anderson, the Fugitive Slave*. Edited by Harper Twelvetrees. 1863. Reprint, New York: Books for Libraries Press, 1971.

Andrews, William L., ed. *African American Autobiography: A Collection of Critical Essays*. Englewood Cliffs, N.J.: Prentice Hall, 1993.

———, ed. *The Oxford Frederick Douglass Reader*. New York: Oxford University Press, 1996.

———. "The Representation of Slavery and the Rise of Afro-American Literary Realism, 1865–1920." In *Slavery and the Literary Imagination*, edited by Deborah

McDowell and Arnold Rampersad, 62–80. Baltimore: Johns Hopkins University Press, 1989.

———, ed. *Sisters of the Spirit: Three Black Women's Autobiographies of the Nineteenth Century*. Bloomington: Indiana University Press, 1986.

———. *To Tell a Free Story: The First Century of Afro-American Autobiography, 1760–1865*. Urbana: University of Illinois Press, 1986.

Andrews, William L., and Mitch Kachun. "Editors' Introduction: The Emergence of Julia C. Collins." In Julia C. Collins, *The Curse of Caste; or, The Slave Bride*, xi–lxviii. 1865; reprint, New York: Oxford University Press, 2006.

Anstey, Roger, and P. E. H. Hair. *Liverpool, the African Slave Trade, and Abolition: Essays to Illustrate Current Knowledge and Research*. Enlarged ed. Liverpool: Historic Society of Lancashire and Cheshire, 1989.

Armstrong, Erica R. "A Mental and Moral Feast: Reading, Writing, and Sentimentality in Black Philadelphia." *Journal of Women's History* 16, no. 1 (2004): 78–102.

Babb, Valerie. *Whiteness Visible: The Meaning of Whiteness in American Literature and Culture*. New York: New York University Press, 1998.

Bailey, John. *The Lost German Slave Girl: The Extraordinary True Story of Sally Miller and Her Fight for Freedom in Old New Orleans*. New York: Atlantic Monthly Press, 2003.

Baldwin, James. "The White Problem." In *The Cross of Redemption: Uncollected Writings*, 72–79, edited by Randall Kenan. New York: Pantheon Books, 2010.

Barclay, Jenifer L. "Coming Full Circle: Harriet Jacobs and the Crafts in Reconstruction-Era Savannah." In *Slavery and Freedom in Savannah*, edited by Leslie M. Harris and Daina Ramey Berry (Athens: University of Georgia Press, 2014), 169–70.

Barrett, Lindon. "Hand-Writing: Legibility and the White Body in *Running a Thousand Miles for Freedom*." *American Literature* 69, no. 2 (June 1997): 315–36.

Bassard, Katherine Clay. *Spiritual Interrogations: Culture, Gender, and Community in Early African American Women's Writing*. Princeton, N.J.: Princeton University Press, 1999.

Bellamy, Donnie D. "Macon, Georgia, 1823–1860: A Study in Urban Slavery." *Phylon* 45, no. 4 (1984): 298–310.

Benjamin, Tritobia Hayes. *The Life and Art of Lois Mailou Jones*. San Francisco: Pomegranate Art Books, 1994.

Berger, Martin A. *Seeing through Race: A Reinterpretation of Civil Rights Photography*. Berkeley: University of California Press, 2011.

Berry, Daina Ramey. *Swing the Sickle for the Harvest Is Ripe: Gender and Slavery in Antebellum Georgia*. Urbana: University of Illinois Press, 2007.

Blackett, Richard J. M. *Beating against the Barriers: The Lives of Six Nineteenth-Century Afro-Americans*. 1986; reprint, Ithaca: Cornell University Press, 1989.

———. *Building an Antislavery Wall: Black Americans in the Atlantic Abolitionist Movement, 1830–1860*. Baton Rouge: Louisiana State University Press, 1983.

———, ed. *Running a Thousand Miles for Freedom; or, The Escape of William and Ellen Craft from Slavery*. 1860; reprint, Baton Rouge: Louisiana State University Press, 1986.

Boggis, JerriAnne, Eva Allegra Raimon, and Barbara A. White, eds. *Harriet Wilson's New England: Race, Writing, and Region*. Durham: University of New Hampshire Press; Lebanon, N.H.: University Press of New England, 2007.

Bordewitch, Fergus M. *Bound for Canaan: The Underground Railroad and the War for the Soul of America*. New York: Amistad, 2005.

Bosman, Julie. "Professor Says He Has Solved a Mystery over a Slave Novel." *New York Times*, September 19, 2013, A1, A3.

The Boston Directory: Containing the City Record, a General Directory of the Citizens, a Special Directory of Trades, Professions, &c., an Almanac, from July, 1849, to July, 1850, with a Variety of Miscellaneous Matter. Boston: George Adams, 1849.

Bowditch, Vincent Y. *Life and Correspondence of Henry Ingersoll Bowditch*. Boston: Houghton Mifflin, 1902.

Boyd, Valerie. *Wrapped in Rainbows: The Life of Zora Neale Hurston*. New York: Scribner's, 2003.

Bradford, Sarah Hopkins. *Harriet Tubman: The Moses of Her People*. 1886; reprint, Bedford, Mass.: Applewood Books, 1993.

Bressey, Caroline. "The Black Presence in England and Wales after the Abolition Act, 1807–1930." *Parliamentary History* 26 (2007): 224–37.

Brooks, Daphne A. *Bodies in Dissent: Spectacular Performances of Race and Freedom, 1850–1910*. Durham, N.C.: Duke University Press, 2006.

Brown, Hallie Quinn. *Homespun Heroines and Other Women of Distinction*. 1926; reprint, New York: Oxford University Press, 1988.

Brown, Lois. "Death-Defying Testimony: Women's Private Lives and the Politics of Public Documents." *Legacy* 27, no. 1 (2010): 130–39.

Brown, William Wells. *The Anti-Slavery Harp: A Collection of Songs for Anti-Slavery Meetings*. Boston: Bela Marsh, 1848.

———. *The Black Man: His Antecedents, His Genius, and His Achievements*. New York: Thomas Hamilton; Boston: R. F. Wallcut, 1863.

———. *Clotel; or, The President's Daughter: A Narrative of Slave Life in the United States*. London: Partridge and Oakey, 1853.

———. *Clotel; or, The President's Daughter: A Narrative of Slave Life in the United States*. Edited by Robert S. Levine. 1853; reprint, Boston: Bedford/St. Martin's, 2000.

———. *The Escape; or, A Leap for Freedom: A Drama in Five Acts*. Edited by John Ernest. Knoxville: University of Tennessee Press, 2001.

———. "A Lecture Delivered before the Female Anti-Slavery Society of Salem." In *William Wells Brown Reader*, edited by Ezra Greenspan, 107–29. Athens: University of Georgia Press, 2008.

———. *Narrative of William W. Brown, A Fugitive Slave*. In *From Fugitive Slave to Free Man: The Autobiographies of William Wells Brown*, edited by William L. Andrews, 27–110. 1848; reprint, New York: Penguin, 1993.

———. "Singular Escape." *Liberator*, January 12, 1849, 7.

Brusky, Sarah. "The Travels of William and Ellen Craft: Race and Travel Literature in the Nineteenth Century." *Prospects* 25 (2000): 177–91.

Burkett, Randall K., Pellom McDaniels III, and Tiffany Gleason. *The Mind of Carter G. Woodson, as Reflected in the Books He Owned, Read, and Published.* Catalog of the Library of Carter G. Woodson and the Association for the Study of African American Life and History. Atlanta: Emory University, 2006.

Campbell, Edward D. C., with Kym S. Rice, eds. *Before Freedom Came: African American Life in the Antebellum South.* Richmond: Museum of the Confederacy and the University Press of Virginia, 1991.

Candler, Allen D., and Clement A. Evans. *Georgia: Comprising Sketches of Counties, Towns, Events, Institutions, and Persons, Arranged in Cyclopedic Form.* Vol. 3. 1900; reprint, Atlanta: State Historical Association, 1906.

Carby, Hazel V. *Reconstructing Womanhood: The Emergence of the Afro-American Woman Novelist.* New York: Oxford University Press, 1987.

Carson, Clayborne, David J. Garrow, Gerald Gill, Vincent Harding, and Darlene Clark Hine, eds. *The Eyes on the Prize Civil Rights Reader: Documents, Speeches, and Firsthand Accounts from the Black Freedom Struggle, 1954–1990.* New York: Penguin Books, 1991.

Chakkalakal, Tess. *Novel Bondage: Slavery, Marriage, and Freedom in Nineteenth-Century America.* Urbana: University of Illinois Press, 2011.

Chamberlain, Allen. *Beacon Hill: Its Ancient Pastures and Early Mansions.* Boston: Houghton Mifflin, 1925.

Chaney, Michael A. *Fugitive Vision: Slave Image and Black Identity in Antebellum Narrative.* Bloomington: Indiana University Press, 2008.

Chapman, Maria Weston. *Songs of the Free and Hymns of Christian Freedom.* Boston: Isaac Knapp, 1836.

Child, Lydia Maria. *The Freedmen's Book.* Boston: Ticknor and Fields, 1865.

———. *The Stars and Stripes: A Melo-Drama.* In *Major Voices: The Drama of Slavery,* edited by Eric Gardner, 443–75. New Milford, Conn.: Toby Press, 2005.

Chirhart, Ann Short, and Betty Wood, eds. *Georgia Women: Their Lives and Times.* Vol. 1. Athens: University of Georgia Press, 2009.

Cima, Gay Gibson. *Performing Anti-Slavery: Activist Women on Antebellum Stages.* Cambridge, UK: Cambridge University Press, 2014.

Clark, George W., comp. *The Liberty Minstrel.* New York: Leavitt and Alden, 1845.

Clarke, James Freeman. *Anti-Slavery Days: A Sketch of the Struggle which Ended in the Abolition of Slavery in the United States.* 1883; reprint, New York: AMS Press, 1972.

Clifton, Lucille. *Good Woman: Poems and a Memoir, 1969–1980.* Rochester, N.Y.: BOA Editions, 1987.

Cohen, Lara Langer, and Jordan Alexander Stein, eds. *Early African American Print Culture.* Philadelphia: University of Pennsylvania Press, 2012.

Collins, Julia C. *The Curse of Caste; or, The Slave Bride.* 1865; reprint, New York: Oxford University Press, 2006.

Collins, Patricia Hill. *Black Feminist Thought: Knowledge, Consciousness, and the Politics of Empowerment.* New York: Routledge, 1990, 2nd ed., 2000.

Collins, Robert. *Essay on the Treatment and Management of Slaves, Written for the Sev-*

enth Annual Fair of the Southern Central Agricultural Society, October, 1852. Macon, Ga.: B. F. Griffin, 1852.

Collison, Gary. *Shadrach Minkins: From Fugitive Slave to Citizen.* Cambridge, Mass.: Harvard University Press, 1997.

Commager, Henry Steele. *Theodore Parker.* Boston: Little, Brown, 1936.

Conry, Jaci. "The Other Beacon Hill." *American Legacy,* Winter 2005, 62–66.

Cowper, William. *The Task and Other Poems.* 1784; reprint, London: Cassell, 1852.

Craft, William. "Primary Education in Georgia," *Boston Daily Advertiser,* August 22, 1873, 2.

Craft, William, and Ellen Craft. *Running a Thousand Miles for Freedom; or, The Escape of William and Ellen Craft from Slavery.* Edited by Barbara McCaskill. Athens: University of Georgia Press, 1999. First published 1860.

———. *Running a Thousand Miles for Freedom; or, The Escape of William and Ellen Craft from Slavery.* Edited by John Ernest. Acton, Mass.: Copley, 2000. First published 1860.

"The Craft Libel Suit." *Boston Daily Advertiser,* June 16, 1878, 2.

"The Craft-Naylor Suit: The Third Day of the Georgia Libel Case." *Boston Daily Advertiser,* June 8, 1878, 2.

Crafts, Hannah. *The Bondwoman's Narrative.* Edited by Henry Louis Gates Jr. Ca. 1853–61; reprint, New York: Time Warner, 2003.

"Crafts v. Schlesinger." *Boston Evening Journal,* July 6, 1878.

Craig, John S., ed. *Craig's Daguerreian Registry.* Torrington, Conn.: J. S. Craig, 1994–96.

Dagbovie, Pero Gaglo. *The Early Black History Movement, Carter G. Woodson, and Lorenzo Johnson Green.* Urbana: University of Illinois Press, 2007.

DeRamus, Betty. *Forbidden Fruit: Love Stories from the Underground Railroad.* New York: Atria Books, 2005.

Dimock, Wai Chee, and Lawrence Buell, eds. *Shades of the Planet: American Literature as World Literature.* Princeton, N.J.: Princeton University Press, 2007.

Directory of the City of Boston: Embracing the City Record, a General Directory of the Citizens, and a Special Directory of Trades, Professions, &c., with An Almanac from July 1850, to July 1851. Boston: George Adams, 1850.

Dodson, Howard, with Amiri Baraka, Gail Buckley, John Hope Franklin, Henry Louis Gates Jr., Annette Gordon-Reed, and Gayraud S. Wilmore. *Jubilee: The Emergence of African-American Culture.* New York: New York Public Library Astor, Lenox and Tilden Foundations; Washington, D.C.: National Geographic, 2002.

Douglass, Frederick. *Life and Times of Frederick Douglass.* In *The Oxford Frederick Douglass Reader,* edited by William L. Andrews, 226–311. New York: Oxford University Press, 1996.

———. *Narrative.* In *Shadowing Slavery, Five African American Autobiographical Narratives,* edited by John Ernest, 1–122. Acton, Mass.: Copley Publishing, 2002.

———. *Narrative of the Life of Frederick Douglass, an American Slave.* Edited by William L. Andrews and William McFeely. 1845; reprint, New York: W. W. Norton, 1997.

————. "Negro Portraits." *Liberator*, April 20, 1849, 18.

Du Bois, W. E. B. *The Philadelphia Negro: A Social Study, Together with a Special Report on Domestic Service, by Isabel Eaton*. Philadelphia: Published for the University, 1899.

————. *The Souls of Black Folk: Essays and Sketches*. Edited by Henry Louis Gates Jr. and Terri Hume Oliver. 1903; reprint, New York: Norton, 1999.

Dugard, Martin. *Into Africa: The Epic Adventures of Stanley and Livingstone*. New York: Doubleday, 2003.

Duitsman, Janet Cornelius. *"When I Can Read My Title Clear": Literacy, Slavery, and Religion in the Antebellum South*. Columbia: University of South Carolina Press, 1991.

Dunbar, Paul Laurence. "We Wear the Mask." In *The Norton Anthology of African American Literature*, 2nd ed., edited by Henry Louis Gates Jr. and Nellie Y. McKay, 918. New York: Norton, 2004.

Early, Gerald L. "The End of Race as We Know It." *The Chronicle Review* 55, no. 7 (October 10, 2008): B13.

Eisenberg, John. *The Great Match Race: When the North Met the South in America's First Sports Spectacle*. Boston: Houghton Mifflin, 2006.

Elizabeth, Charlotte. "The Slave and Her Babe." In *The Liberty Minstrel*, comp. George W. Clark (New York: Leavitt and Alden, 1845), 13.

Ellis, Douglas T. "City of Richmond Hill, Bryan County, Georgia." In *The History of Bryan County, 1793–1985*. Bryan County, Ga.: Bryan County Historical Society, 1986, 7–11.

Emberton, Carole. "It's (Still) a Man's World: Gendering Freedom in the Civil War Era." Public lecture, Miller Learning Center, University of Georgia, Athens, October 23, 2013.

Ernest, John. *Chaotic Justice: Rethinking African American Literary History*. Chapel Hill: University of North Carolina Press, 2009.

————. *Liberation Historiography: African American Writers and the Challenge of History, 1794–1861*. Chapel Hill: University of North Caroline Press, 2004.

————. "Representing Chaos: William Crafts' *Running a Thousand Miles for Freedom*." *PMLA* 121, no. 2 (2006): 469–83.

————, ed. *Shadowing Slavery: Five African American Autobiographical Narratives*. Acton, Mass.: Copley, 2002.

"An Ex-Slave's Reminiscences." *Indianapolis Sentinel*, January 3, 1882, 7.

Fabian, Ann. *The Unvarnished Truth: Personal Narratives in Nineteenth-Century America*. Berkeley: University of California Press, 2002.

Fairclough, Adam. *To Redeem the Soul of America: The Southern Christian Leadership Conference and Martin Luther King, Jr*. Athens: University of Georgia Press, 2001.

Farrison, William. *William Wells Brown, Author and Reformer*. Chicago: University of Chicago Press, 1969.

Fauset, Jessie. *Quicksand*. In *An Intimation of Things Distant: The Collected Fiction of Nella Larsen*, edited by Marita Golden, 29–162.

"The Feeling in the South: The Emancipated Slaves." *Glasgow Herald*, December 12, 1878, 3.

The Fifth Exhibition of the Massachusetts Charitable Mechanic Association, at Faneuil and Quincy Halls, in the City of Boston, September 1847. Boston: Dutton and Wentworth, 1847.

Fisch, Audrey A. *American Slaves in Victorian England: Abolitionist Politics in Popular Literature and Culture.* Cambridge, UK: Cambridge University Press, 2000.

———, ed. *The Cambridge Companion to the African American Slave Narrative.* Cambridge, UK: Cambridge University Press, 2007.

Five Hundred Thousand Strokes for Freedom: A Series of Anti-Slavery Tracts, of which Half a Million Are Now First Issued by the Friends of the Negro. Leeds Anti-Slavery Society, 1853.

Foreman, Pier Gabrielle. "Who's Your Mama? 'White' Mulatta Genealogies, Early Photography, and Anti-Passing Narratives of Slavery and Freedom." *American Literary History* 14, no. 3 (2002): 505–39.

———, and Reginald H. Pitts. Introduction to *Our Nig; or, Sketches from the Life of a Free Black, Living in a Two-Story White House, North, Showing that Slavery's Shadows Fall Even There.* By Harriet E. Wilson. 1859; reprint, New York: Penguin, 2005, xxiii–l.

Foster, Frances Smith. "African American Progress-Report Autobiographies." In *Redefining American Literary History*, edited by A. LaVonne Brown Ruoff and Jerry Ward Jr., 270–84. New York: Modern Language Association, 1990.

———, ed. *A Brighter Coming Day: A Frances Ellen Watkins Harper Reader.* New York: Feminist Press at the City University of New York, 1990.

———. "Creative Collaboration: As African American as Sweet Potato Pie." In McCaskill and Gebhard, *Post-Bellum, Pre-Harlem*, 17–33.

———. "A Narrative of the Interesting Origins and (Somewhat) Surprising Developments of African-American Print Culture." *American Literary History* 17, no. 4 (2005): 714–40.

———. *'Til Death or Distance Do Us Part: Marriage and the Making of African America.* New York: Oxford University Press, 2010.

———. *Witnessing Slavery: The Development of the Ante-Bellum Slave Narratives*, 2nd ed. Westport, Conn.: Greenwood Press, 1994.

———. *Written by Herself: Literary Production by African American Women, 1746–1892.* Bloomington: Indiana University Press, 1996.

The Fourth Exhibition of the Massachusetts Charitable Mechanic Association at Quincy Hall, in the City of Boston, Sept. 16, 1844. Boston: Crocker and Brewster, 1844.

Fox, Stephen. *Transatlantic: Samuel Cunard, Isambard Brunel, and the Great Atlantic Steamships.* New York: HarperCollins, 2003.

Fox-Genovese, Elizabeth. *Within the Plantation Household: Black and White Women of the Old South.* Chapel Hill: University of North Carolina Press, 1988.

Fradin, Judith Bloom, and Dennis Brindell Fradin. *5,000 Miles to Freedom: Ellen and William Craft's Flight from Slavery.* Washington, D.C.: National Geographic Society, 2006.

Franklin, John Hope, and Alfred A. Moss Jr. *From Slavery to Freedom: A History of African Americans*, 8th ed. New York: McGraw-Hill, 2000.

Freedman, Florence B. *Two Tickets to Freedom: The True Story of William and Ellen Craft, Fugitive Slaves*. New York: P. Bedrick Books, 1989.

Freeman, JoyEllen. "A Portrayal of Power: Black Nationalism in the Documentary *Now Is the Time*." Master's thesis, University of Georgia, 2011.

Frothingham, Octavius Brooks. *Theodore Parker: A Biography*. Boston: J. R. Osgood, 1874.

"The Fugitive Slave Bill and its Effects." In *Five Hundred Thousand Strokes for Freedom*, 1–12, 92.

Fulton, DoVeanna S. *Speaking Power: Black Feminist Orality in Women's Narratives of Slavery*. Albany: State University of New York Press, 2006.

———, and Reginald Pitts, eds. *Speaking Lives, Authoring Texts: Three African American Women's Oral Slave Narratives*. Albany: State University of New York Press, 2010.

Gardner, Eric. "African American Cultures of Print." Summer Seminar on the History of the Book, American Antiquarian Society, Worcester, Massachusetts, July 20, 2012.

———, ed. *Major Voices: The Drama of Slavery*. New Milford, Conn.: Toby Press, 2005.

———. "Of Bottles and Books: Reconsidering Readers of *Our Nig*." In *Harriet Wilson's New England*, edited by JerriAnne Boggis, Eve Allegra Raimon, and Barbara A. White, 3–26. Durham: University of New Hampshire Press; Lebanon, N.H.: University Press of New England, 2007.

———. "Remembered (Black) Readers: Subscribers to the *Christian Recorder*, 1864–1865." *American Literary History* 23, no. 2 (2011): 229–59.

———. "'This Attempt of Their Sister': Harriet Wilson's *Our Nig* from Printers to Readers." *New England Quarterly* 66, no. 2 (1993): 226–46.

———. *Unexpected Places: Relocating Nineteenth-Century African American Literature*. Jackson: University Press of Mississippi, 2009.

Gates, Henry Louis, Jr. *Figures in Black: Words, Signs, and the "Racial" Self*. New York: Oxford University Press, 1989.

———. "James Gronniosaw and the Trope of the Talking Book." In *African American Autobiography: A Collection of Critical Essays*, edited by William L. Andrews, 8–25. Englewood Cliffs, N.J.: Prentice Hall, 1993.

Gates, Henry Louis, Jr., and Nellie Y. McKay, eds. *The Norton Anthology of African American Literature*, 2nd ed. New York: Norton, 2004.

Gerzina, Gretchen Holbrook. *Black London: Life before Emancipation*. New Brunswick, N.J.: Rutgers University Press, 1995.

———, ed. *Black Victorians, Black Victoriana*. New Brunswick, N.J.: Rutgers University Press, 2003.

Gerzina, Gretchen Holbrook, with Anthony Gerzina. *Mr. and Mrs. Prince: How an Extraordinary Eighteenth-Century Family Moved Out of Slavery and into Legend*. New York: Amistad, 2008.

Goggin, Jacqueline. *Carter G. Woodson: A Life in Black History*. Baton Rouge: Louisiana State University Press, 1991.

Golden, Marita, ed. *An Intimation of Things Distant: The Collected Fiction of Nella Larsen*. New York: Doubleday, 1992.

Goldfield, David R. "Black Life in Old South Cities." In *Before Freedom Came: African American Life in the Antebellum South*, edited by Edward D. C. Campbell and Kym S. Rice, 128–53. Richmond: Museum of the Confederacy and the University Press of Virginia, 1991.

Gould, Philip. "The Rise, Development, and Circulation of the Slave Narrative." In Fisch, *Cambridge Companion to the African American Slave Narrative*, 11–27.

Graham, Maryemma, and Jerry W. Ward Jr., eds. *The Cambridge History of American Literature*. Cambridge, UK: Cambridge University Press, 2011.

Greenspan, Ezra. *William Wells Brown: A Reader*. Athens: University of Georgia Press, 2008.

Grimes, William. *Life of William Grimes, the Runaway Slave*. New York: W. Grimes, 1825.

Grimké, Archibald. "Anti-Slavery in Boston." *New England Magazine* 3, no. 4 (1890): 441–59.

Grover, Kathryn. *The Fugitive's Gibraltar: Escaping Slaves and Abolitionism in New Bedford, Massachusetts*. Amherst: University of Massachusetts Press, 2001.

Guralnick, Peter. *Dream Boogie: The Triumph of Sam Cooke*. New York: Little, Brown, 2005.

———. *Sweet Soul Music: Rhythm and Blues and the Southern Dream of Freedom*. New York: Harper and Row, 1986.

Hacker, J. David. "A Census-Based Count of the Civil War Dead." *Civil War History* 57, no. 4 (2011): 307–48.

Hahn, Steven. *A Nation under Our Feet: Black Political Struggles in the Rural South, from Slavery to the Great Migration*. Cambridge, Mass.: Belknap Press of Harvard University, 2003.

Hall, James C., ed. *Approaches to Teaching the Narrative of the Life of Frederick Douglass*. New York: Modern Language Association of America, 1999.

Harris, Leslie M., and Daina Ramey Berry, eds. *Slavery and Freedom in Savannah*. Athens: University of Georgia Press, 2014.

Hayden, Robert C. *African Americans in Boston: More than 350 Years*. Boston: Trustees of the Public Library of the City of Boston, 1991.

Hayden, Robert C., and the staff of the Museum of Afro-American History. *The African Meeting House in Boston: A Celebration of History*. Boston: Companion Press, 1987.

Haywood, Chanta M. *Prophesying Daughters: Black Women Preachers and the Word, 1823–1913*. Columbia: University of Missouri Press, 2003.

Heglar, Charles J. *Rethinking the Slave Narrative: Slave Marriage and the Narratives of Henry Bibb and Ellen Craft*. Westport, Conn.: Greenwood Press, 2001.

Hine, Darlene Clark. "Carter G. Woodson: White Philanthropy and Negro Historiography." *History Teacher* 19, no. 3 (1986): 405–25.

Hoffman, Charles, and Tess Hoffman. *North by South: The Two Lives of Richard Arnold*. Athens: University of Georgia Press, 2009.

Horton, James Oliver, and Lois E. Horton. *Black Bostonians: Family Life and Community Struggle in the Antebellum North*. New York: Holmes and Meier, 1979.

Hoyle, Pamela. *The Development of Photography in Boston, 1840–1875*. Boston: Boston Athenæum, 1979.

Hull, Gloria T., Patricia Bell Scott, and Barbara Smith, eds. *All the Women Are White, All the Blacks Are Men, but Some of Us Are Brave: Black Women's Studies*. Old Westbury, New York: Feminist Press, 1982.

Hunter, Tera W. *"To 'Joy My Freedom": Southern Black Women's Lives and Labors after the Civil War*. Cambridge, Mass.: Harvard University Press, 1997.

Hurston, Zora Neale, and Langston Hughes. *Mule Bone: A Comedy of Negro Life*. New York: Harper Perennial, 2008.

Jackson, Leon. "The Talking Book and the Talking Book Historian: African American Cultures of Print—The State of the Discipline." *Book History* 13 (2010): 251–308.

Jacobs, Harriet A. *Incidents in the Life of a Slave Girl*. Enlarged ed. Edited by Jean Fagan Yellin. 1861; reprint, Cambridge, Mass.: Harvard University Press, 2000.

Jones, Jacqueline. *Labor of Love, Labor of Sorrow: Black Women, Work, and Family from Slavery to Freedom*. New York: Basic Books, 1985.

Jones, Norrece T., Jr. "Rape in Black and White: Sexual Violence in the Testimony of Enslaved and Free Americans." In *Slavery and the American South: Essays and Commentaries*, edited by Winthrop D. Jordan, 93–108. Jackson: University Press of Mississippi, 2003.

Joseph, Peniel E. *Waiting 'Til the Midnight Hour: A Narrative History of Black Power in America*. New York: Henry Holt, 2006.

Kaplan, Carla. *Zora Neale Hurston: A Life in Letters*. New York: Anchor, 2003.

Karcher, Carolyn L. *The First Woman of the Republic: A Cultural Biography of Lydia Maria Child*. Durham, N.C.: Duke University Press, 1998.

Keetley, Dawn. "Racial Conviction, Racial Confusion: Indeterminate Identities in Women's Slave Narratives and Southern Courts." *A/B: Autobiography Studies* 10, no. 2 (1995): 1–20.

King, Deborah K. "Multiple Jeopardy, Multiple Consciousness: The Context of a Black Feminist Ideology." In *Black Women in America: Social Sciences Perspectives*, edited by Micheline R. Malson, Elisabeth Mudimbe-Boyi, Jean F. O'Barr, and Mary Wyer, 265–95. Chicago: University of Chicago Press, 1988.

Law, Robin. *Ouidah: The Social History of a West African Slaving 'Port,' 1727–1892*. Athens: Ohio University Press; Oxford: James Currey, 2004.

Lemke, Donald B. *The Brave Escape of William and Ellen Craft*. Mankato, Minn.: Capstone Press, 2006.

Levine, Robert S. Introduction to *Clotel; or, The President's Daughter*, by William Wells Brown, 3–27. 1853; reprint, Boston: Bedford/St. Martin's, 2000.

Levy, Valerie Domenica. *The Antislavery Web of Connection: Maria Weston Chapman's Liberty Bell, 1839–58*. PhD diss., University of Georgia, 2002.

"The Libel Suit. The Romantic Story of a Runaway Slave." *Boston Daily Advertiser*, June 17, 1878, 4.

Lord, Priscilla Sawyer, and Virginia Clegg Gamage. *Marblehead: The Spirit of '76 Lives Here*. Philadelphia: Chilton, 1972.

Lott, Eric. *Love and Theft: Blackface Minstrelsy and the American Working Class*. New York: Oxford University Press, 1993.

Maffly-Kipp, Laurie F. *Setting Down the Sacred Past: African-American Race Histories*. Cambridge, Mass.: Belknap Press of Harvard, 2010.

Martin, Waldo E., Jr. *No Coward Soldiers: Black Cultural Politics and Postwar America*. Cambridge, Mass.: Harvard University Press, 2005.

McCaskill, Barbara. "Ellen Craft (ca. 1826–1891): The Fugitive Who Fled as a Planter." In Chirhart and Wood, *Georgia Women*, 82–105.

———. "Introduction: William and Ellen Craft in Transatlantic Literature and Life." In *Running a Thousand Miles for Freedom*, by William and Ellen Craft, vii–xxv. Athens: University of Georgia Press, 1999.

———. "'Trust No Man!' But What about a Woman? Ellen Craft and a Genealogical Model for Teaching Douglass's *Narrative*." In *Approaches to Teaching the Narrative of the Life of Frederick Douglass*, edited by James C. Hall, 95–101. New York: Modern Language Association of America, 1999.

———. "'Yours Very Truly': Ellen Craft—The Fugitive as Text and Artifact." *African American Review* 28, no. 4 (1994): 509–29.

McCaskill, Barbara, and Caroline Gebhard, eds. *Post-Bellum, Pre-Harlem: African American Literature and Culture, 1877–1919*. New York: New York University Press, 2006.

McCluskey, Audrey Thomas. "'Manly Husbands and Womanly Wives': The Leadership of Educator Lucy Craft Laney." In McCaskill and Gebhard, *Post-Bellum, Pre-Harlem*, 74–88.

McCoy, Beth A. "Race and the (Para)textual Condition," *PMLA* 121, no. 1 (2006): 156–69.

McDaniels, Pellom, III. "The Prophetic Vision of Carter Godwin Woodson." In *The Mind of Carter G. Woodson, as Reflected in the Books He Owned, Read, and Published*, by Burkett, Randall K., Pellom McDaniels III, and Tiffany Gleason, 25–42. Atlanta: Emory University, 2006.

McDowell, Deborah, and Arnold Rampersad, eds. *Slavery and the Literary Imagination*. Baltimore: Johns Hopkins University Press, 1989.

McHenry, Elizabeth. *Forgotten Readers: Recovering the Lost History of African-American Literary Societies*. Durham, N.C.: Duke University Press, 2002.

McMillan, Uri. "Ellen Craft's Radical Techniques of Subversion," *e-misférica* 5, no. 2 (Winter 2008), http://hemisphericinstitute.org/hemi/en/e-misferica-52/mcmillan.

McReady, Elredge J. "Wedding Feast in N.Y. Celebrates 1850 Marriage of Macon Slave Couple." *Macon Metro Times*, November 13–19, 1991, 1.

McWorter, Gerald. "The Nature and Needs of the Black University." In *The Eyes on the Prize Civil Rights Reader: Documents, Speeches, and Firsthand Accounts from the*

Black Freedom Struggle, 1954–1990, edited by Clayborne Carson, David J. Garrow, Gerald Gill, Vincent Harding, and Darlene Clark Hine, 470–79. New York: Penguin Books, 1991.

Meer, Sarah. *Uncle Tom Mania: Slavery, Minstrelsy, and Transatlantic Culture in the 1850s.* Athens: University of Georgia Press, 2005.

Midgley, Clare. *Women Against Slavery: The British Campaign, 1780–1870.* London: Routledge, 1992.

Millette, HollyGale. "Exchanging Fugitive Identity: William and Ellen Craft's Transatlantic Reinvention (1850–69)." In *Imagining Transatlantic Slavery*, edited by Cara Kaplan and John Oldfield, 61–75. Houndmills, UK: Palgrave Macmillan, 2010.

"Mr. William Craft and His School." *Boston Daily Advertiser*, October 4, 1876.

"Mr. William Craft's Mission to Dahomey: Letter from Mr. William Craft." *Caledonian Mercury*, July 3, 1863, 3.

Moody, Joycelyn. *Sentimental Confessions: Spiritual Narratives of Nineteenth-Century African American Women.* Athens: University of Georgia Press, 2001.

Moore, Cathy. *The Daring Escape of William and Ellen Craft.* Minneapolis: Carolrhoda Books, 2002.

Mossell, Gertrude N. F. *The Work of the Afro-American Woman.* 1894; reprint, New York: Oxford University Press, 1988.

Mulvey, Christopher. "Freeing the Voice, Creating the Self: The Novel and Slavery." In *The Cambridge Companion to the African American Novel*, edited by Maryemma Graham, 17–33. Cambridge, UK: Cambridge University Press, 2004.

"A Notable Case: Libel Suit of William Craft against Naylor & Co." *Boston Daily Advertiser*, June 6, 1878, 2.

O'Connor, Thomas. *Eminent Bostonians.* Cambridge, Mass.: Harvard University Press, 2002.

Olney, James. "'I Was Born': Slave Narratives—Their Status as Autobiography and Literature." In *The Slave's Narrative*, edited by Charles T. Davis and Henry Louis Gates, Jr., 148–74. New York: Oxford University Press, 1985.

Pachai, Bridglal, and Henry Bishop. *Historic Black Nova Scotia.* Halifax, N.S.: Nimbus, 2006.

Paine, Robert Treat. *The Works, in Verse and Prose, of the Late Robert Treat Paine, Jun. Esq., with Notes to Which Are Prefixed Sketches of His Life, Character and Writings.* Boston: J. Belcher, 1812.

Painter, Nell Irvin. *The History of White People.* New York: W. W. Norton, 2010.

———. *Sojourner Truth: A Life, a Symbol.* New York: Norton, 1997.

Parker, Theodore. *Ten Sermons of Religion.* 1853; reprint, Boston: Ticknor and Fields, 1861.

———. *The Trial of Theodore Parker for the "Misdemeanor," or a Speech in Faneuil Hall against Kidnapping, before the Circuit Court of the United States.* Boston, T. Parker, 1855.

Penn, Irving Garland. *The Afro-American Press and Its Editors.* Springfield, Mass.: Willey, 1891.

Peterson, Carla L. *"Doers of the Word": African American Women Speakers and Writers in the North (1830–1880)*. New York: Oxford University Press, 1995.

Petrulionius, Sandra Harbert. *To Set This World Right: The Antislavery Movement in Thoreau's Concord*. Ithaca: Cornell University Press, 2006.

Pettit, Clare. *Dr. Livingstone, I Presume? Missionaries, Journalists, Explorers, and Empire*. Cambridge, Mass.: Harvard University Press, 2007.

Pierce, Yolanda. "Redeeming Bondage: The Captivity Narrative and the Spiritual Autobiography in the African American Slave Narrative Tradition." In Fisch, *The Cambridge Companion to the African American Slave Narrative*, 83–98.

Polito, Ronald. *A Directory of Boston Photographers, 1840–1900*. 2nd ed. Boston: University of Massachusetts Press, 1983.

Powell, Timothy B. *Ruthless Democracy: A Multicultural Interpretation of the American Renaissance*. Princeton, N.J.: Princeton University Press, 2002.

Pressly, Paul M. *On the Rim of the Caribbean: Colonial Georgia and the British Atlantic World*. Athens: University of Georgia Press, 2013.

Raimon, Eva Allegra. *The 'Tragic Mulatta' Revisited: Race and Nationalism in Nineteenth-Century Antislavery Fiction*. New Brunswick, N.J.: Rutgers University Press, 2004.

Ray, Emma. *Twice Sold, Twice Ransomed: Autobiography of Mr. and Mrs. L. P. Ray*. Chicago: Free Methodist Publishing House, 1926.

Reid-Pharr, Robert. *Conjugal Union: The Body, the House, and the Black American*. New York: Oxford University Press, 1999.

———. "The Post-Bellum Race Novel." In *The Cambridge Companion to the American Novel*, edited by Leonard Cassutto, Clare Virginia Eby, and Benjamin Reiss, 470–83. Cambridge, UK: Cambridge University Press, 2011.

Richards, Jeffrey H. *Drama, Theatre, and Identity in the American New Republic*. Cambridge, UK: Cambridge University Press, 2005.

Richardson, Marilyn, ed. *Maria W. Stewart: America's First Black Woman Political Writer: Essays and Speeches*. Bloomington: Indiana University Press, 1987.

Robbins, Sarah. *The Cambridge Introduction to Harriet Beecher Stowe*. Cambridge, UK: Cambridge University Press, 2007.

Roediger, David, ed. *John Brown*. New York: Modern Library, 2001.

Rowell, Charles H. "An Interview with Lois Mailou Jones." *Callaloo: A Journal of African and African American Arts* 12, no. 2 (Spring 1989): 357–78.

Ruggles, Jeffrey. *The Unboxing of Henry Brown*. Charlottesville: University of Virginia Press, 2003.

Ruoff, A. LaVonne Brown, and Jerry Ward, Jr., eds. *Redefining American Literary History*. New York: Modern Language Association, 1990.

Ryan, Barbara. "Old and New Issue Servants: 'Race' Men and Women Weigh In." In McCaskill and Gebhard, *Post-Bellum, Pre-Harlem*, 89–100.

Samuels, Ellen. "'A Complication of Complaints': Untangling Disability, Race, and Gender in William and Ellen Craft's *Running a Thousand Miles for Freedom*." *MELUS* 31, no. 3 (2006): 15–47.

Sanborn, Geoffrey. "The Plagiarist's Craft: Fugitivity and Theatricality in *Running a Thousand Miles for Freedom.*" *PMLA* 128, no. 4 (2013): 907–22.

Sekora, John. "Black Message/White Envelope: Genre, Authenticity and Authority in the Antebellum Slave Narrative." *Callaloo: A Journal of African and African American Arts* 10 (Summer 1987): 482–515.

The Seventh Exhibition of the Massachusetts Charitable Mechanic Association, at Faneuil and Quincy Halls, in the City of Boston, September, 1853. Boston: Damrell and Moore and George Coolidge, 1853.

Shaw, Gwendolyn DuBois. "Landscapes of Labor: Race, Religion, and Rhode Island in the Painting of Edward Mitchell Bannister." In McCaskill and Gebhard, *Post-Bellum, Pre-Harlem,* 59–73.

———. *Portraits of a People: Picturing African Americans in the Nineteenth Century.* Andover, Mass.: Addison Gallery of American Art, Phillips Academy; Seattle: University of Washington Press, 2006.

Sichel, Kim. *Black Boston: Documentary Photography and the African American Experience.* Boston: Boston University Gallery, 1994.

Siebert, Wilbur H. *The Underground Railroad from Slavery to Freedom.* New York: Macmillan, 1898.

———. *The Underground Railroad in Massachusetts.* Worcester, Mass.: American Antiquarian Society, 1936.

"Singular Escapes from Slavery." In *Five Hundred Thousand Strokes for Freedom,* 4–8.

The Sixth Exhibition of the Massachusetts Charitable Mechanic Association, at Faneuil and Quincy Halls, in the City of Boston, September, 1850. Boston: Eastburn's Press, 1850.

Smith, Jennifer Lund. "Lucy Craft Laney and Martha Berry (1855–1933; 1866–1942)." In Chirhart and Wood, *Georgia Women,* 318–40.

Stephens, Judith L., ed. *The Plays of Georgia Douglas Johnson: From the New Negro Renaissance to the Civil Rights Movement.* Urbana: University of Illinois Press, 2006.

Sterling, Dorothy. "Ellen Craft: The Valiant Journey." In *Black Foremothers: Three Lives,* 2nd ed., 3–59. Old Westbury, N.Y.: Feminist Press, 1988.

———. *We Are Your Sisters: Black Women in the Nineteenth Century.* New York: Norton, 1984.

Stevenson, Brenda E. *Life in Black and White: Family and Community in the Slave South.* New York: Oxford University Press, 1996.

Still, William. *The Underground Rail Road: A Record of Facts, Authentic Narratives, Letters, &c., Narrating the Hardships, Hair-Breadth Escapes, and Death Struggles of the Slaves in Their Efforts for Freedom, as Related by Themselves and Others or Witnessed by the Author: Together with Sketches of Some of the Largest Stockholders and Most Liberal Aiders and Advisers of the Road.* Philadelphia: Porter and Coates, 1872.

———. "William and [Ellen] Craft: Female Slave in Male Attire, Fleeing as a Planter, with Her Husband as Her Body-Servant," *San Francisco Elevator,* December 7, 1872, 3.

Stowe, Harriet. *Uncle Tom's Cabin; or, Life among the Lowly*. 2nd ed. Edited by Elizabeth Ammons. 1852; reprint, New York: W. W. Norton, 2010.

Sullivan, Buddy. "Black Education in Bryan, 1865–1875: William and Ellen Craft at Woodville." In *From Beautiful Zion to Red Bird Creek: History of Bryan County, Georgia, Including Chronicles of the Old Canoochee-Ogeechee River Country*, 201–3. Bryan County, Ga.: Bryan County Board of Commissioners, 2000.

Tatham, David. *Winslow Homer and the Pictorial Press*. Syracuse, N.Y.: Syracuse University Press, 2003.

Thomas, Rhondda Robinson. *Claiming Exodus: A Cultural History of Afro-Atlantic Identity, 1740–1903*. Waco, Texas: Baylor University Press, 2013.

Twain, Mark. *The Adventures of Tom Sawyer*. Edited by Beverly Lyon Clark. New York: W. W. Norton, 2007. First published 1876.

"Two Schools for Negroes." *New York Evening Post*, January 3, 1876, 2.

Von Frank, Albert. *The Trials of Anthony Burns: Freedom and Slavery in Emerson's Boston*. Cambridge, Mass.: Harvard University Press, 1999.

Voss, Frederick S. *Majestic in His Wrath: A Pictorial Life of Frederick Douglass*. Washington, D.C.: Smithsonian Institution Press, 1995.

Walker, Alice. *In Search of Our Mothers' Gardens: Womanist Prose*. New York: Harcourt Brace Jovanovich, 1983.

Wallace, Maurice O. *Constructing the Black Masculine: Identity and Ideality in African American Men's Literature and Culture, 1775–1995*. Durham, N.C.: Duke University Press, 2002.

Ward, Geoffrey C., and Ken Burns. *Jazz: A History of America's Music*. New York: Alfred A. Knopf, 2000.

Wardrop, A. Daneen. "Collaboration in *Running a Thousand Miles for Freedom*: William's Key and Ellen's Renaming." *Arizona Quarterly* 61, no. 3 (2005): 57–73.

———. "Ellen Craft and the Case of Salomé Muller in *Running a Thousand Miles for Freedom*." *Women's Studies* 33, no. 7 (2004): 961–84.

Washington, Booker T. *The Story of the Negro: The Rise of the Race from Slavery*. Vol. 1. New York: Doubleday, 1909.

———. *Up from Slavery: An Autobiography*. Edited by William L. Andrews. New York: Oxford University Press, 1995. First published 1901.

Waters, Kristin, and Carol B. Conaway, eds. *Black Women's Intellectual Traditions: Speaking Their Minds*. Burlington: University of Vermont Press, 2007.

Weinauer, Ellen. "'A Most Respectable Looking Gentleman': Passing, Possession, and Transgression in *Running a Thousand Miles for Freedom*." In *Passing and the Fictions of Identity*, edited by Elaine K. Ginsberg, 37–56. Durham, N.C.: Duke University Press, 1996.

Weiss, John, ed. *Life and Correspondence of Theodore Parker*. 2 vols. New York: D. Appleton, 1864.

White, Deborah Gray. *Ar'n't I a Woman? Female Slaves in the Plantation South*. 1985; reprint, New York: W. W. Norton, 1987.

Wilder, Craig Steven. *Race, Slavery and the Troubled History of America's Universities*. New York: Bloomsbury, 2013.

"William Craft." *Boston Daily Advertiser*, March 4, 1879, 2.

"William Craft and His School." *Boston Daily Advertiser*, October 4, 1876, 2.

Williams, Heather Andrea. "'Clothing Themselves in Intelligence': The Freedpeople, Schooling, and Northern Teachers, 1861–1871." *Journal of African American History* 87 (2002): 372–89.

——. *Help Me to Find My People: The African American Search for Family Lost in Slavery*. Chapel Hill: University of North Carolina Press, 2012.

——. *Self-Taught: African American Education in Slavery and Freedom*. Chapel Hill: University of North Carolina Press, 2005.

Williams, James. *Life and Adventures of James Williams, a Fugitive Slave; with a Full Description of the Underground Railroad*. San Francisco: Women's Union Print, 1873.

Willis, Deborah. *Reflections in Black: A History of Black Photographers, 1840 to the Present*. New York: W. W. Norton, 2000.

——. "The Sociologist's Eye: W. E. B. Du Bois and the Paris Exposition." In *A Small Nation of People: W. E. B. Du Bois and African American Portraits of Progress*, by the Library of Congress, 51–78. New York: Amistad, 2003.

Willis, Deborah, and Barbara Krauthamer. *Envisioning Emancipation: Black Americans and the End of Slavery*. Philadelphia: Temple University Press, 2013.

Wilson, Carol. *The Two Lives of Sally Miller: A Case of Mistaken Identity in Antebellum New Orleans*. New Brunswick, N.J.: Rutgers University Press, 2007.

Wilson, Harriet E. *Our Nig; or, Sketches from the Life of a Free Black, Living in a Two-Story White House, North, Showing that Slavery's Shadows Fall Even There*. 3rd ed. Edited by Henry Louis Gates Jr. 1859; reprint New York: Vintage, 3rd ed., 2002. First published 1859.

Winks, Robin W. *The Blacks in Canada: A History*. Montreal: McGill-Queens University Press, 1971.

Wood, Marcus. *Blind Memory: Visual Representations of Slavery in England and America, 1780–1865*. Manchester, UK: Manchester University Press, 2000.

Woodson, Carter Godwin. "Letters to Antislavery Workers and Agencies [Part 5]." *Journal of Negro History* 10, no. 4 (1925): 749–74.

——, ed. *The Mind of the Negro as Reflected in Letters Written during the Crisis, 1800–1860*. 1926; reprint Washington, D.C.: Association for the Study of Negro Life and History, 2006.

——. "The Thrilling Escape of William and Ellen Craft." *Negro History Bulletin* 1, no. 1 (1937), 1, 5.

Yee, Shirley J. *Black Women Abolitionists: A Study in Activism, 1828–1860*. Knoxville: University of Tennessee Press, 1992.

Yellin, Jean Fagan. *Harriet Jacobs: A Life*. New York: Basic Civitas, 2004.

——, ed. *The Harriet Jacobs Family Papers*. Vol. 1. Chapel Hill: University of North Carolina Press, 2008.

——. Introduction to *Incidents in the Life of a Slave Girl*, by Harriet Jacobs, xv–xliii. Edited by Jean Fagan Yellin. Cambridge, Mass.: Harvard University Press, 2000.

————. *Women and Sisters: The Antislavery Feminists in American Culture*. New Haven, Conn.: Yale University Press, 1989.

Zackodnik, Teresa C. "The Enslaved as Spectacle: Ellen Craft, Sarah Parker Remond, and American Slavery in England." *Nineteenth-Century Prose* 29, no. 1 (2002): 78–102.

————. *The Mulatta and the Politics of Race*. Jackson: University of Mississippi Press, 2004.

————. *Press, Platform, Pulpit: Black Feminist Politics in the Era of Reform*. Knoxville: University of Tennessee Press, 2011.

Zafar, Rafia. *We Wear the Mask: African Americans Write American Literature, 1760–1870*. New York: Columbia University Press, 1997.

Index

Aberdeen Journal (newspaper), 70

African American communities: in Boston, 35–36, 85; and early photography, 37–38; early print culture in, 10–12; stereotyping of, 83

African Meeting House (Boston), 28, 35

Allen, Marlene D., 9

A. M. E. Book Concern (publishing house), 10

A. M. E. Christian Recorder (journal), 10

American Anti-Slavery Society, 44. *See also* Child, Lydia Maria; *Liberty Bell*

American Eclipse (horse), 32

American Missionary Association, 12

American Revolution, African Americans in, 52–53

Ampadu, Lena, 3

Andrews, Benedict, 67

Andrews, James, 80. *See also* Craft, Ellen; Craft, William

Andrews, Joseph (engraver), 40, 42. *See also* Craft, Ellen

Andrews, William L., 3, 12

antislavery communities: in Boston, 35–36, 85; in Halifax, Nova Scotia, 52, 98n56. *See also* Underground Railroad

Appleton, George, 80. *See also* Craft, Ellen; Craft, William

Arnold, Richard, in history of Woodville Cooperative Farm School, 80. *See also* Craft, Ellen; Craft, William

Baldwin, James, 1–2

Bassard, Katherine Clay, 3

Bellamy, Donnie D., 26

Beloved (Morrison), 90

Bibb, Henry, 52. *See also* Underground Railroad

Bishop, Henry, 53

Black Arts Movement, 6–7

Blackett, Richard J. M., biography of the Crafts, 5, 19

Bond, Hannah, 48, 98n42

Bondwoman's Narrative, The (Bond), 48, 98n42

Boone, Sherry, 89. *See also* Craft, Ellen

Bordewitch, Fergus M., 37

Boston Daily Advertiser (newspaper), 80–81, 83, 85. *See also* Craft, Ellen; Craft, William

Bowditch, William Ingersoll: at libel trial of William Craft, 84; as Underground Railroad conductor, 50. *See also* Underground Railroad

Brave Escape of William and Ellen Craft, The (Lemke), 8–9

Bristol Mercury (newspaper): on the Crafts and William Wells Brown, 70; on William Craft at antislavery meeting, 71–72. *See also* Craft, Ellen; Craft, William

Brown, Henry "Box," 31; in public exhibitions of escape from slavery, 69, 103n54

Brown, John, 67

Brown, Josephine (daughter of William Wells Brown), 25

Brown, Lois, 11, 51

Brown, William Wells, 39, 44, 103n59; on antislavery stage with the Crafts, 6, 36, 70, 89; as coauthor of the Crafts' memoir, 59, 100n3; depiction of the Crafts in *Clotel*, 48, 98n43; depiction of enslaved mother, 29–30; treatment as slave, 61

Bunch, Lonnie, 105n24

Burns, Anthony, 28. *See also* Fugitive Slave Law

Caledonian Mercury (newspaper), 72–74

Cambria (steamship): treatment of Douglass on, 54; voyage of the Crafts to Liverpool on, 53–55

Chakkalakal, Tess, 62, 92

Chapman, Maria Weston, 40. See also *Liberty Bell*

Chesson, Frederick William, 73–74

Child, Lydia Maria, 43–44, 100n2; on the Crafts' character, 86; discussion of the Crafts in *The Freedmen's Book*, 70–71; in libel suit of William Craft, 79, 84; story of the Crafts in *Stars and Stripes*, 43–48

Christian Slave, The (Stowe), 43

Cima, Gay Gibson, 36–37

Civil War: and the Crafts' return to Georgia, 6; photography of, 37; and publication of *Running a Thousand Miles for Freedom*, 67

Clarke, James Freeman: on Ellen Craft's baby, 28–29; at libel trial of William Craft, 84; as supporter of Woodville School, 79; in Vigilance Committee, 50

Clifton, Lucille, 91–92

Clinton, Georgia, 18

Clotel (Brown), 48, 98n43, 103n59

Collins, Robert: as businessman, 22–23; letter to President Fillmore, 62–63; opinions

about slave marriages, 62–63. *See also* Fugitive Slave Law

Cornelius, Janet Duitsman, 26

Cornwallis Street African Baptist Church (Halifax), 53

Cowper, William, 47, 92, 106n17

Craft, Alfred (son), 39, 78 (fig. 8)

Craft, Alice Isabella Ellen (daughter; Mrs. William Demosthenes Crum), 39, 77 (Fig. 7), 87

Craft, Charles Estlin Phillips (son), 39, 76 (Fig. 6), 84

Craft, Ellen, 11, 14, 34–35, 55–56, 75–76, 85–86; on antislavery stage, 36–37, 42–43, 70; in Boston, 35–37, 42–43, 48–52; childhood of, 18–19; children of, 29, 39, 76 (Fig. 6), 77 (Fig. 7), 78 (fig.8), 96n4; in Clinton (Ga.), 18; as coauthor of *Running a Thousand Miles for Freedom*, 5, 100n3; in England, 65, 66–67, 70, 81–82, 90; engraving and daguerreotype in masculine disguise, 37, 38–43, 41 (Fig. 4), 58–59; escape from slavery, 16 (Fig. 1), 24–27, 31–33, 48, 65, 68–69, 92; fictional treatments of, 5, 8–9, 15–18, 44–48; and Fugitive Slave Law, 50, 51–52; grandson of, 87–88; in Halifax, Nova Scotia, 52–54, 66, 99n56; infant, death of, 27–30; libel suit, testimony in, 82–84; literacy of, 25–26, 36; in Macon, Georgia, 21–31; in marriage, 24–25, 27–28, 30–31, 50–52, 62–63, 92; memory of, 6, 88–92; mother of, 18–19, 27, 59–60; at Ockham School, 65, 81–82, 83; photograph of, 21 (Fig. 3); public letter of, 102n38; sister (white), 18–19; as target of Fugitive Slave Law, 50, 62–63; treatment during slavery, 18–19, 23, 58, 95n21; on voyage to Liverpool, 56; at Woodville Cooperative Farm School, 79, 82–83. *See also specific works about William and Ellen Craft*

Craft, Henry Kempton (grandson), 87–88

Craft, Mary Elizabeth (daughter), 29

Craft, Stephen Brougham Dennoce (son), 39, 84

Craft, William, 11, 14, 34–35, 55–56, 75–76; on antislavery stage, 36; in Boston, 35–37, 42–43, 48–52; children of 27–31, 39–40, 76 (Fig.

6), 77 (Fig. 7), 78 (Fig. 8), 94n4; as coauthor of *Running a Thousand Miles for Freedom*, 5, 59, 100n3; in England, 65, 66–70, 81–82, 90, 104n68; escape from slavery, 16 (Fig. 1), 24–27, 33–34, 65, 92; fictional treatments of, 5, 8–9, 15–18, 16 (Fig. 1), 44–48; and Fugitive Slave Law, 50, 51–52; as fundraiser for Hickory Hill and Woodville Cooperative Farm School, 77– 82, 86; grandson of, 87–88; in Halifax, Nova Scotia, 52–54, 66, 99n56; libel suit, testimony in, 80–85; literacy of, 25–26, 36; in Macon, Georgia, 21–31; marriage to Ellen, 24–25, 27–28, 30–31, 50–52, 62–63, 92; memory of, 6, 88–92; at Ockham School, 64, 65, 81–82, 83, 104n68; photograph of, 19, 20 (Fig. 2); physical appearance of, 19–21; separation from mother, father, brother, and sister, 22, 28, 58; treatment by owners, 26–27, 58; Whydah, travel to, 70–74, 76. *See also specific works about William and Ellen Craft*

Craft, William II (son), 39

Crafts, Hannah. *See* Bond, Hannah

Crum, William Demosthenes (son-in-law), 87

Cunard Line: prejudice against African American passengers, 54, 66; route from Halifax to Liverpool, 54

Davis, Ossie, 7

Dee, Ruby, 7

Deeper Wrong, The (Jacobs), 60

Delamotte, Charles, 104n6

Dodge, Betsey, 52. *See also* Underground Railroad

Dodge, Simeon, 52. *See also* Underground Railroad

Douglass, Frederick, 20; on antislavery stage with the Crafts, 38; as Cunard Line passenger, 54, 55, 100n1; on new name in freedom, 32; treatment during slavery, 61

Ellen Craft: A New American Story (Boone), 89

"Ellen Craft: The Valiant Journey" (Sterling), 5, 19, 23–24

Ellis, Rufus, 79. *See also* Society for the Propagation of the Gospel

Escape, The: or, A Leap for Freedom (Brown), 44

Essay on the Management and Treatment of Slaves (Collins), 22, 62–63

Estlin, John Bishop, 67–68

Fabian, Ann, 42

Fillmore, Millard, 48, 63. *See also* Collins, Robert

Flynn, Katherine E., 29, 96n4

Foreman, Gabrielle P., 3; on early African American texts, 8; on the Crafts' race pride, 21

Foster, Frances Smith, 3; on early African American marriages and families, 62; on early African American print culture, 10, 57; on collaborations in early African American literature, 5

Freedmen's Book, The (Child), 43–44, 70–71

Fugitive Slave Law, 49 (Fig. 5); Crafts, impact on, 63–64; passage of, 48–49; in *The Underground Rail Road*, 86. *See also* Underground Railroad

fugitive slaves: agency of, 35, 42–43; in Boston, 36; in Halifax, Nova Scotia, 52–54; stories, influence of, 7–8, 86, 87–92

Fulton, DoVeanna, 3

Gardner, Eric: on collaborations in early African American literature, 91; on early African American print culture, 10–11; on slave narratives, 60–61

Garrison, William Lloyd: conflict with Frederick Douglass, 20; at libel trial of William Craft, 79, 84; as publisher of *Liberator*, 36

Gates, Henry Louis, Jr., 3

Generations (Clifton), 91

Georgia Telegraph (newspaper), 19

Gould, Philip, 57; on veracity of fugitives' stories, 61–62

Greenspan, Ezra: on Craft's friendship with William Wells Brown, 6; on source of *Clotel* (Brown), 103n59

Grimes, William, 56–57

Grover, Kathryn: on free African Americans posing as fugitive slaves, 105n12; on photograph of William Craft, 19

Guardian (newspaper), 88

Hahn, Stephen: hiring out of slaves, 26–27; literacy of slaves, 26

Hale, Edward Everett: at libel trial of William Craft, 84; as supporter of Woodville School, 79

Hale, Luther Holman, 40, 42. See also Craft, Ellen

Halifax, Nova Scotia: antislavery community in, 53–54, 99n56; the Crafts' escape to, 52, 53–54, 64, 66; as refuge for fugitives from slavery, 52–53. See also Craft, Ellen; Craft, William

Harper, Frances Ellen Watkins, 29, 100n2

Hayden, Lewis: at marriage of the Crafts, 40, 50–51; as mentor to the Crafts, 35, 40; as Underground Railroad conductor, 35; in Vigilance Committee, 64. See also Underground Railroad

Haywood, Chanta M., 3

Henson, Josiah, 52. See also Stowe, Harriet Beecher

Hickory Hill, Georgia, 78

Hillard, George Stillman, 81; as supporter of Woodville school, 79

hiring out, 26–27

Horton, James Oliver, 35, 50

Horton, Lois E., 35–50

Hughes, Langston, 2

Hughes, Willis: pursuit of Crafts, 49–50, 52, 67; tangles with abolitionists, 50, 52. See also Vigilance Committee

Hurston, Zora Neale, 2, 3–4, 8

Incidents in the Life of a Slave Girl (Jacobs), 60, 61, 64

intersectional match races, 32

Ivens, Barkley, 64, 102n46. See also Quakers

Jackson, Leon, 10–11

Jacobs, Harriet: memoir, 60, 64; treatment in slavery, 61

Johnson, Georgia Douglas, 5

"Johnson, William" (pseudonym of Ellen Craft), 31–32

Jones, Lois Mailou, 17

Jones, Norrece T., Jr., 18

Joseph, Peniel E., 6–7

King, George P., 80–81, 104n9

Knight, John: pursuit of the Crafts, 49–50, 52, 67; tangles with abolitionists, 50, 52. See also Vigilance Committee

Leeds Mercury (newspaper), 70

Lemke, Donald B., 8–9

Liberator (newspaper), 20, 36, 40; article by Douglass, 38

Liberty Bell (journal), 40, 44

Life of William Grimes, 56–57

Liverpool, 55–56, 66

Loring, Ellis Gray, 50

Loyalists, Black, 53

Macon, Georgia: home of the Crafts, 18–19, 21–24; the Crafts' escape from, 24–27, 31–33, 48, 65, 68–69, 92. See also Collins, Robert

Maffly-Kipp, Laurie, 91

Martin, Waldo E., Jr., 6–7

Martineau, Harriet, 76

Massachusetts Charitable Mechanic Association, 40

May, Samuel, 67–68

McCaskill, Barbara: discussion of Ellen Craft, 4–5; public letter of Ellen Craft, 102n38. See also Craft, Ellen

McCoy, Beth A., 12

McHenry, Elizabeth, 12

Meer, Sarah, 30

Middle Passage, 90

Millette, HollyGale: class affiliation of the Crafts, 81–82, 105n14; public exhibitions of fugitive slaves, 69

Monroe and Bibb Railroad and Banking Company, 22. See also Collins, Robert

Moody, Joycelyn, 3

Morris, Robert: and libel suit, 85; in Vigilance Committee 50, 64

Morrison, Toni, Beloved, 90

Müller, Salomé, 58, 101n15

National Anti-Slavery Standard (newspaper), 43

Naylor and Company, 80, 104n9. See also Craft, Ellen; Craft, William

Negro History Bulletin (journal), 16 (Fig. 1);

fictional treatment of the Crafts' escape, 15–19; publication history and goals of, 14–15, 95n4

Nell, William Cooper, 50

New Negro Renaissance, 2, 6–7

Now Is the Time (television documentary), 7

Ockham School, 64, 65, 81–82, 83, 104n68. *See also* Craft, Ellen; Craft, William

"Odyssey of William and Ellen Craft, The" (Blackett), 5, 19

Our Nig (Wilson), 81

Pachai, Bridglal, 53

Painter, Nell Irvin, 37

paratext, definition of, 12

Parker, Theodore, 96n4; on Ellen's baby, 28–29; at marriage of the Crafts, 40, 50–51; in Vigilance Committee, 50. *See also* Vigilance Committee

Peterson, Carla L., 3

Phillips, Wendell: libel trial, testimony in, 84; as supporter of Woodville school, 84

Picquet, Louisa, 58

Pierce, Yolanda, 3

Pitts, Reginald, 3, 8

Powell, Timothy B., 92

Preston, Richard, 53

Provincial Freeman (newspaper), 3

Purvis, Robert, 64, 102n40

Quakers: and the Crafts' escape from slavery, 64, 102n46; and the Crafts' memoir, 60, 102n46

Ray, Emma, 56–57

Ray, L. P., 56–57

Reid-Pharr, Robert, 9

Richards, Jeffrey H., 20–21

Running a Thousand Miles for Freedom (Craft and Craft), 3, 103n59; antislavery communities in, 65–68, 69–70; authorship of, 59, 100n3; discussion of Fugitive Slave Law, 49; editions, 60, 95n20; England, praise of, 36, 65, 67–68; escape from slavery in, 24–27, 31, 32–33, 103n58; marriage in, 23, 62; production and marketing of, 58–61; slav-

ery, discussions of, 23–26, 27–28; themes of, 9, 57–58, 62, 65–66. *See also* Craft, Ellen; Craft, William

Saltonstall, Leverett, 81

Sanborn, Geoffrey, 59, 100n3

Schlesinger, B., accusations against William Craft, 80–81, 104n9. *See also* Naylor and Company

Schlesinger, Sebastian Barthold, 80–81, 104n9. *See also* Naylor and Company

Schoff, Stephen Alonzo, 40, 42

Schomburg Center for Research in Black Culture, 1–2

Sewall, Samuel Edmund: as supporter of Woodville School, 79; testimony in libel suit, 85

Shadd, Mary Ann, 52

Shaw, Gwendolyn DuBois, 38

Sichel, Kim, 38

slave narratives, 3; reception of, 61; in recovery of early African American literature, 7–8; themes of, 9, 56–58, 88–90

slavery: division of labor, 57; fictional treatments of, 5, 8–9, 15–18, 29–30, 44–48; fugitives from, 36, 52–54; Fugitive Slave Law, 48–49; literacy rates in, 26; marriages in, 24–28, 30–31; memories of, 6–8, 19, 88–92; rape and sexual violence, 18, 57, 61–62

Smith, James P., 80, 81

Smith, Maria, 18, 19, 59–60

Society for the Propagation of the Gospel, 12, 79

Sterling, Dorothy, 5, 19, 23

Stevenson, Brenda E., 34

Still, William, 15, 85–86

Stowe, Harriet Beecher: *The Christian Slave*, 43; *Uncle Tom's Cabin*, 15, 30, 40, 42, 48, 52

Taylor, Ira H., 22

Trotter, Elizabeth Letitia, 88

Twain, Mark, 8–9

Tweedie, William, 60–61

Twice Sold, Twice Ransomed (Ray), 56–57

Uncle Tom's Cabin (Stowe): fictionalization of the Crafts' escape, 48, 52; in letter of

Uncle Tom's Cabin (Stowe) (*continued*)
William Craft, 15; marketing with Ellen's engraving, 40, 42; motherhood in, 30
Underground Railroad: in Boston, 35, 84; in Canada, 52–53; involvement in the Crafts' escape, 27, 64, 102n46
Underground Rail Road, The (Still), 15, 85–86

Vigilance Committee, 50, 64
Voice of the Fugitive (newspaper), 52

Walker, Alice, 8
Ward, Samuel Ringgold, 52. *See also* Underground Railroad
Wardrop, Daneen, 103n58
War of 1812, African Americans in, 52–53
Washington, Booker T., 87
Webb, Mary E., 43
White, Deborah Gray, 57
Whittier, John Greenleaf, 20
Whydah, correspondence of William Craft from, 71–74, 76. *See also* Craft, William

William and Ellen Craft (Johnson), 59
Williams, Heather Andrea, 59
Williams, James, 14
Williams, Seretha D., 9
Willis, Deborah, 37
Wilson, Harriet E., 81
Wood, Marcus, 39
Woodson, Carter Godwin, 5, 14; fictional treatment of the Crafts, 15–19. See also *Negro History Bulletin*
Woodville Cooperative Farm School (Woodville School): as center of libel suit, 80–85; conditions of, 82–83; demise of, 86; fundraising for, 77–78, 79, 83–85; purpose of, 78–79. *See also* Craft, Ellen; Craft, William

Yellin, Jean Faga, 64, 104n65

Zackodnik, Teresa C.: on engraving of Ellen Craft, 39, 42–43; on fugitive slaves' agency, 42–43
Zafar, Rafia, 3, 89